Ancient Peoples and Places
THE PARTHIANS

General Editor
DR GLYN DANIEL

ABOUT THE AUTHOR

Malcolm Colledge studied Classics at St John's College, Cambridge. In 1961 he held the University Walston Studentship, and he has spent several years travelling and living in various countries of the Mediterranean and the Middle East, in order to pursue his studies in the archaeology of Parthian Iran and the eastern Roman provinces. He has taken part in excavations in Britain, Jordan and Iran. Formerly Lecturer in Classics, Ancient History and Classical Archaeology at the University College of Swansea, he now lectures in the same subjects at Westfield College, University of London.

Ancient Peoples and Places

THE
PARTHIANS

Malcolm A. R. Colledge

76 PHOTOGRAPHS
46 LINE DRAWINGS
2 MAPS
1 TABLE

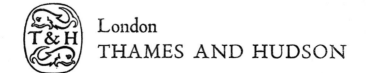

London
THAMES AND HUDSON

THIS IS VOLUME FIFTY-NINE IN THE SERIES

Ancient Peoples and Places

GENERAL EDITOR: DR GLYN DANIEL

FIRST PUBLISHED 1967
PRINTED IN HOLLAND BY
KONINKLIJKE DRUKKERIJ G. J. THIEME N.V., NIJMEGEN
NOT TO BE IMPORTED FOR SALE INTO THE U.S.A.

CONTENTS

ILLUSTRATIONS

7

To Margaret and Bronwen

Preface

IF THE 'PARTHIAN SHOT' has become proverbial, the Parthians themselves have not achieved a comparable fame. Readers of the leading poets and historians of ancient Rome will
have come across references to this mysterious eastern people
beyond the Euphrates river. They will remember the tremendous defeat of Crassus by the Parthian horse-archers at Carrhae,
and the sufferings of Corbulo's soldiers in the snows of Armenia. It is striking that these major classical writers are almost
unanimous in their hostility towards their eastern neighbours.
The Parthians emerge from their pages as treacherous, bellicose
and arrogant barbarians with curious and distasteful customs.
This picture is, however, manifestly owed to propaganda, of
which Romans were adept producers. Who were the Parthians
in fact, of what kind was their civilisation, and why was all
this hostility engendered?

In trying to produce some of the answers, I have aimed at giving, so far as is possible, a rounded picture of the Parthians.
Excavation is contributing more to knowledge of this people
every year, and adding to the comparatively scanty information
provided by ancient writings. More space than is usual in this
series has been devoted to Parthian political history, as this is
rarely found in other books and much of it in any case is drawn
from archaeological sources. In transliterating Greek and oriental words and names, I have tried to respect tradition and simplicity as well as accuracy. As regards the problems of Zoroastrian religion in this period, I follow the modern school of
thought which considers that the prophet's teaching was gradually adopted into the religious beliefs of Iran. Through the
archaeological researches of the past forty years it is now possible
to give some account of Parthian architecture and art, which

13

were previously more or less unknown and until very recently quite misunderstood. But questions in plenty remain to be answered concerning this people, particularly while so many Parthian cities lie completely unexplored.

I am most grateful to the directors and staff of the many museums and institutions which have given me assistance over a number of years and permission now to reproduce material in their possession. Many others have given timely aid toward the preparation of the book, including Antran Evan, Theresa Goell, Rustam Kavoussi, Mrs Moghadam, Julian Reade, John Staley, David Stronach and Professor J. M. C. Toynbee. My thanks go also to Dr Glyn Daniel and the staff of Thames and Hudson, and to H. A. Shelley for drawing the maps so skilfully from my sketches. Blemishes which remain are of course my own responsibility.

At best, the book provides only a sketch of the Parthians. Those who wish to delve deeper will have to rummage in the Bibliography for the keys to further information. But I hope very much that some readers at least will find profit, and even entertainment, in this introduction to a complex and still elusive civilisation.

M.A.R.C.

CHAPTER I

Geography and Records

IN ANTIQUITY, THE SUPERBLY SCENIC mountain ranges and the deserts of Iran formed natural barriers to movement and communication so stupendous that, inevitably, the activities of inhabitants and invaders alike were channelled along certain routes and into certain areas. The high and rocky central plateau of Iran consists largely of two enormous salt deserts, the Dasht-i Kavir and the Dasht-i Lut, and is ringed with mountains that not infrequently exceed ten thousand feet in height. To the east rises the Hindu Kush, to the north the Elburz range, to the north-west the mountains of Azerbaijan and the Caucasus, and to the west the Zagros chain which overlooks the broad plains of Mesopotamia. To the north-east and to the south-west, Iran is bordered by lower and kinder lands. Around the Caspian Sea lie coastal stretches where a rich and exotic vegetation flourishes, although these lands quickly degenerate as one travels north-eastwards into the harsher steppes of Turkmenistan and the habitat of the central Asian nomads. To the south-west lies the richest land of all, the immensely fertile alluvial plain of the rivers Tigris and Euphrates. This was one of the areas where primitive society first produced a food surplus, and for millennia it remained a prize which outsiders sought to seize and dominate. Over most of the Iranian lands, rainfall is scarce. The temperatures vary considerably, from great heat in the plains and deserts during summer to bitter cold in the upland and mountain winters. Across eastern Iran every summer blows the terrible Wind of One Hundred and Twenty Days.

Such was the geographical mould into which the actions of the people of western Asia were pressed. The Iranian mountain ring could be crossed by large groups of people only

Fig. 1

Plate 2

through a limited number of passes. The presence of extensive deserts hampered free movement further. So the invaders who, at intervals, entered Iran from the lands north-east of the Caspian were forced by the existence of the salt deserts to turn either west into Iran or south-east into Afghanistan and India. Traders who wished to cross Iran carrying goods from the Mediterranean to China perforce followed an ancient track, later known as the Silk Route, which ran north of the Iranian deserts to Bactria, and then turned north-east to cross central Asia by the oases. As for the inhabitants, much of the terrain is suitable only for a nomadic existence. Settled populations grew up in the few plains watered by rivers or lakes, in the more productive river valleys, and around the oases that dotted the wastes. Farming was often hard and involved irrigation, and all over Iran systems of underground canals were built to preserve the water. The only important area not to require irrigation was the north-western province of Azerbaijan (Atropatene), where extensive and comparatively fertile plains supported a considerable farming population.

These conditions have remained constant factors in the history of Iran since the invasions by Iranian horsemen of the territories of 'greater Iran', the useful modern term for the Iranian cultural area in antiquity. The very word 'Iran' embodies the name of the Aryan occupants of the land. Persia was the classical Greek equivalent of the name of the Achaemenid province of Parsa, the modern Fars. Owing to the extension of the meaning of Persia to include the whole of Iran, it is better to distinguish the province by its later title Persis. Parthia too was a term first applied by classical and early Hellenistic Greek authors to an Achaemenid satrapy, that of Parthava. When the group of Iranian Parni nomads with whom we are concerned entered the province of Parthia, they came to be regarded as 'Parthians' by Greek and Roman writers. After their conquest of the whole of 'greater Iran' the term expanded in meaning with the Empire, and it is necessary to distinguish between the satrapy and the kingdom of the same name.

The Parthians themselves have left scarcely any written records of their existence. Parthian coins therefore form the most valuable extant official documents of the dynasty, and they, like the majority of the few surviving official records, are inscribed normally in Greek. But numerous documents of their subjects survive, inscriptions, parchments and clay records, found predominantly in the western Parthian regions and written in cuneiform, Aramaic, Greek and occasionally Parthian, Latin and Hebrew. Although these documents are usually concerned with local matters, they do at times record facts of importance.

Fortunately, this rather scanty information can be supplemented by a large number of passages and references which are scattered astonishingly widely through the works of Greek and Latin writers. These authors know little of the first century of Parthian history, and those who refer to this period, Polybius, Strabo, Justin and Arrian, mostly lived long after the event and have little to say in any case. But from 141 BC, the year in which the Parthians occupied Babylonia, their history begins to be better known. Obviously, the writers who are most to be relied upon are those who knew Parthia personally. The Greek Apollodorus from Artemita east of the Tigris, the historian used by Trogus Pompeius (whose own work survives only in Justin's epitome), the writer who recorded the Parthian view of Crassus' disaster at Carrhae, these were such men. Their works are lost, but were used, sometimes extensively, by Strabo, Justin, Plutarch and others whose books have been preserved. Justin's epitome of Trogus, however, provides the only connected account of earlier Parthian history. Isidorus from Spasinu Charax, at the head of the Persian Gulf, must have been another who knew parts of Parthia personally. His little work, the *Parthian Stations,* survives. In it he lists the important stopping-places along the main overland route across Iran. Modern scholarship

Fig. 1 The provinces of the Parthian Empire and surrounding territories

ORASMIA

MASSAGETAE

R. Jaxartes

SACARAUCAE

SOGDIANE

APAVARTIKENE
•Nisa
ASTAUENE
PARTHIA
PARTHYENE
TAPURIA
TRAXIANE?

MARGIANE

R. Oxus

BACTRIA

PAROPANISADAE

GANDHARA

•Taxila

ARIA

an

SACASTANE
(DRANGIANE)

R. Helmand

ARACHOSIA

t

'SCYTHIA'

R. Indus

NIA

GEDROSIA

INDIA

-H.A.S-

19

has convicted him of deception. He includes certain provinces in eastern Iran as within the Parthian realm, apparently unaware that they had been lost to the Parthians for at least a century in his own day. He must have compiled his list from a survey dating back to around 100 BC. But in spite of these shortcomings, to which many ancient writings are all too prone, his guide book remains extremely valuable.

The letters of Cicero, the poems of Horace, the work of Velleius Paterculus and the *Stratagems* of Frontinus all contain references to contemporary Parthia. These, like the large majority of Western writers of the Roman period, tend to take a hostile view. Early contacts between Parthians and Romans were frequently unhappy, and frontier disputes prevented these early wounds from healing. Thus the more extensive passages about Parthia and Rome to be found in Tacitus, Plutarch and Dio Cassius are concerned all too often with military campaigns. Many other historians contribute passages and facts, among whom may be noted Appian, Arrian, Herodian, Fronto, the followers of Livy, the biographer Suetonius, and the writers of the Augustan history. But most of these writers were reproducing information which they had obtained at second or third hand, and wherever possible their acounts have to be checked against other evidence. Philostratus' life of the philosopher and mystic Apollonius of Tyana, who went on a lengthy journey across Parthia in the mid first century AD, seems pure fiction at first reading, but never ceases to surprise by the amount of latent fact that it contains. Lucian's passages about Mesopotamia are unfortunately trivial, although he actually originated from a town of the region, Samosata. Lastly, the Sibylline Oracles contribute some information, particularly those composed after the event.

Oriental writings are also informative. Of these, the Jewish, the Syriac and the Chinese are the best, as they are all either contemporary with the events described or based on contemporary accounts. The Talmud throws some light on relations between Jews and Parthians, and one of the most reliable historians of the period is the short-sighted Jew who wrote in Greek, Josephus. Syriac writers used good sources often actually written under Parthian rule. From the second century BC onwards, Chinese travellers and traders began to reach Parthia and to take back information and reports of events that were intimately connected with the history of Iran. Their accounts are sober and valuable, and would be still more so if further correspondences could be found between the names in Chinese and Western sources.

Later Oriental accounts are not so helpful. Knowledge of the Parthians was rapidly lost or destroyed after the fall of their dynasty. Armenian writers such as Moses of Chorene tend towards serious inaccuracy and even sheer fantasy. The Arab historians and geographers have disappointingly little to say of historical value. The books and commentaries of the Zoroastrian religion contain some relevant information. But by the time of the Persian writers and poets of the ninth and tenth centuries AD, the real history of the Parthians was forgotten, and legends were accepted as historical fact. Thus the great Persian epic concerning the rulers of Iran from earliest times, the *Shahnameh* or Book of Kings of Firdosi, has far less to record of the Parthians than Homer has of the Mycenaeans. Delightful in themselves, the legends of the Arabs and Persians, it must be admitted, have little to offer the seeker after historical truth.

Chapter II

The Coming of the Parni

THE TRIPLE DEFEAT inflicted by Alexander the Great upon Darius III (336–330 BC), the last ruler of the Achae-menid Empire, and the establishment of Hellenistic Greek rule in the wake of the conqueror, proved to be a turning-point in the history of western Asia. In the flames of Persepolis the old world was consumed. The arrival and settlement of Mace-donian and Greek soldiers in Asia could not but work deep changes in the life and society of Mesopotamia and Persia. Alexander himself had conceived the idea of fusing the Greek and Oriental elements in his newly-won empire and took prac-tical steps to this end. In his government, Iranians were given the highest appointments along with Greeks. Veteran soldiers were settled in new colonies, and intermarriage was encouraged. After Alexander's sudden death in 323 BC, his generals began to fight for portions of the empire. In the ensuing struggles be-tween the rival Diadochi, or Successors, Alexander's distin-guished general Seleucus remained in the forefront of events. His earlier lack of success was reversed by his entry into Baby-lon in the autumn of 312 BC. From this date were reckoned the years of a 'Seleucid' era. During the next decade, Seleucus re-pulsed the attacks of his rivals and built up an Oriental empire which stretched from Mesopotamia to Afghanistan, with a new capital at Seleucia on the Tigris. The battle of Ipsus, fought in 301 BC, confirmed Seleucus' hold on his possessions, to which he added not only Syria and a further capital at An-tioch on the Orontes, but eventually Asia Minor as well.

The administration which he and his son, the first Antiochus, set up owed much to that of the Achaemenids. The great sat-rapies survived, subdivided into perhaps seventy-two eparchies and these into hyparchies. Taxation seems to have functioned

Fig. 1

basically as before, with great variety in the methods adopted in different parts. Weights and measures were not disturbed, but the Seleucids introduced the Attic Greek system side by side with the older. Local religions were not only tolerated but sometimes even encouraged. The Seleucid kings themselves took over the position of the Achaemenid monarch as absolute ruler, and their power depended to a dangerous extent upon their personality. To many of their subjects, they were the object of reverence. The king owned all land, apparently including temple land, with the exception of that owned by free cities. He ruled, principally through his court and supported by his army and bureaucracy, over a multitude of cities, tribes and vassal kingdoms, and the rulers of the latter usually had their own courts on the royal model. But if the Seleucids theoretically owned almost all the land in their empire, this did not mean that they wielded effective control over all their possessions. Their primary concerns were with Syria and Mesopotamia, where their capitals were founded, and with the great route across the empire from Mesopotamia to Bactria, along which communications and trading were maintained. Regions outside these areas were subject to less control or even to none. Seleucid possessions were held chiefly by the settlement of veteran soldiers and other Greeks in colonies placed at strategic positions. The creation of these settlements fostered an enduring loyalty among the Greeks to the Seleucid dynasty, a loyalty which became an important factor in later times of stress. The colonies were of differing size and status, but their functions were the same: to preserve and defend the Seleucid Empire. Inevitably, as they were centres of Greek culture, these towns in time exercised a strong Hellenising influence around them. Greek language and law, and even Greek art, were often adopted or absorbed to a greater or lesser extent into the local cultures of Iran and Mesopotamia. Thus Alexander's aim of fusion began to become a reality under the Seleucids, if not with their enthusias tic support. Seleucus himself had a Sogdian wife, and Iranian blood therefore ran in the veins of his successors. The effects of the fusion between Hellenic and Oriental which now began lasted well beyond the downfall of the Seleucid dynasty.

The foundation of the capital cities of Seleucia and then Antioch in the far west of the Seleucid Empire underlines the lopsided character of the realm and the unequal interests of the rulers. Moreover, the ancient historians who dealt with Seleucid affairs were mainly concerned with wars against the rulers of Egypt and other Hellenistic kingdoms. With so much to occupy them in the west, the Seleucids inevitably neglected the east. Strabo pinpoints this weakness when he says of Seleucid government in Hyrcania that they ruled it for a short time, but, involved in wars as they were, they could not attend to their further territories. The centring of interest and administration upon the west, however, had its advantages. The losses of whole sections of the eastern territories could be sustained without the collapse of the central government. The Seleucids could scarcely have foreseen, however, that the defection of the distant satrapy of Parthia was ultimately to contribute greatly to their own ruin.

By the middle of the third century BC, the situation in the eastern Seleucid satrapies was becoming tense. The north-eastern borders were constantly threatened by the danger of nomad invasion from central Asia. Yet the satraps were forced to waste valuable resources in assisting the central government in a war against Egypt. Other factors were at work. Jealousies between Greeks and Macedonians and the promptings of personal ambition all contributed to spur on the satraps to seize their independence. The situation was made all the more dangerous by the presence in the area of the semi-nomadic Iranian tribe of the Parni. When a leader of character, Arsaces, appeared among the tribe, the stage was set for the first act. What happened next is related variously by the ancient sources. The accounts range from a sober if jejune narrative to a romance of reprehensible passion. As the two early accounts of Strabo and Trogus (in Justin's epitome) are not only credible but agree against the later group, it is better to reconstruct the events upon the basis of what they say. The outbreak of a bitter civil war in the west in 245 BC, which involved hostilities with Egypt, gave the satrap of Parthia, probably Andragoras by name, the opportunity to revolt. This defection was followed by that of Diodotus, governor of Bactria, probably in 239 BC. Meanwhile Arsaces and the Parni had been watching events. The defeat of the reigning monarch Seleucus II by Celtic invaders at Ancyra about 238 BC opened the way for Arsaces to eject Andragoras and occupy the province of Parthia. An entire Seleucid satrapy was now in Iranian hands.

The tribe of the Parni (or Aparni), which was now assuming such importance in Seleucid affairs, was according to Strabo and Trogus one of three tribes in the small confederacy of the Dahae, which lived on the eastern side of the Caspian sea. The Parni seem to have moved into the regions of Parthia and perhaps also Bactria after the death of Alexander the Great, when disturbances occurred among the tribes of south Russia. Once established, they appear to have lived in a semi-nomadic state, and their language became mixed with the local one. The founder of the Arsacid dynasty, Arsaces himself (or Arshak in Parthian), is mentioned on an inscribed potsherd found at Nisa in Russian Turkestan, an early Parthian town. Arsaces was therefore a historical figure, although tradition romanticised his accession as king of the Parni. Subsequent practice, moreover, made of his name a title used by succeeding kings, like Caesar and Augustus among the Romans, but to the exclusion of their personal names, so that identification of individual monarchs is often difficult, especially on the coins. The Parthians later used an era for reckoning years imitated from the Seleucid, but which began with 247 BC – the year of Arsaces' accession?

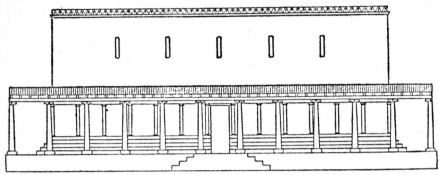

Fig. 2   The façade of the mausoleum, Nisa. Earlier Parthian period (after Vestnik Drevnei Istorii, *1953, 3, fig. 4)*

The first years of the Parthian state were occupied with fighting and with the annexation of some of Hyrcania. Arsaces perished during this period, and according to later classical tradition his brother the second Arsaces then became king, a type of succession with parallels in other Iranian societies. This brother allegedly bore the personal name Tiridates, although some historians doubt the attribution. A capital was built at Dara on mount Apaortenon, a site now identified near Abi-vard and vividly described by Justin as both impregnable and beautiful, and surrounded by fertile lands, streams and woods excellent for hunting. Concerning this early period, Isidorus adds that 'Arsaces' (perhaps the founder of the line) was crown-ed at Asaak in Astauene, part of the satrapy of Parthia, and

Fig. 2

Fig. 3

that the royal necropolis was situated at Nisa (or Parthaunisa). On this site, now in Russian Turkestan, substantial buildings have been excavated, and inscribed documents and a looted treasury found, but the royal tombs have not yet been located. The second Arsaces' position was not a strong one, but two pieces of good fortune ensured the survival of his kingdom. Firstly the Seleucid monarch Seleucus II was too much occupied with fighting in the west to attend to this revolt, and secondly an alliance was arranged with Diodotus, son and successor of

Fig. 3 Marble statuette, probably of a goddess, from Nisa. About 1 : 2. Second century BC *(after* Union Soviétique, *December 1954)*

the rebel satrap of Bactria. So 'Tiridates' had time to organise his kingdom and build up his army before the expected punitive expedition of Seleucus II. This did not take place until about 228 BC. 'Tiridates' was forced to retreat north-eastwards before Seleucus into the distant steppes of the Apa-saca or Water Saca tribes of central Asia. But Seleucus was hastily recalled to Antioch to settle further internal troubles, leaving the Parthians masters of their terrain. The fact, however, that none of the early Parthian monarchs issued any coins of their own, but used Seleucid issues, would suggest that they all stood in an official relationship with the Seleucids which presumably represented some form of vassaldom.

No further event is known until after 217 BC, when 'Tiridates' occupied Hyrcania and Comisene, thus gaining the rich lands around the south-east coast of the Caspian. He now moved his capital to the Seleucid city of Hecatompylus, a site as yet undiscovered but which lay on the main trade route across Iran. At his death about 211 BC, his son, apparently the first Artabanus, became king. By 209 the Parthians held territory which stretched perhaps as far as Ecbatana in Media, but this was the moment when Seleucus' successor Antiochus III became free to regain the rebel provinces. In a lengthy campaign he retook Ecbatana, chased away the Parthian horsemen sent by Artabanus to destroy the precious underground canals beside the salt desert, and entered Hecatompylus with ease. Then he fought his way through fierce opposition across Tapuria in the eastern Elburz, reconquered Hyrcania, and finally made an alliance with Artabanus. Antiochus completed his success by forcing Euthydemus of Bactria also to recognise his supremacy. Then, in order to confirm the restoration of order in the east,

27

Antiochus marched on, following the route of Alexander the Great through the Hindu Kush, over the Khyber Pass into the Punjab, and finally returned through Seistan and Kerman to Seleucia on the Tigris. The kingdom of Parthia had been reduced in size by his expedition, but it had survived.

Parthia may shortly have suffered further territorial losses through an attack by the king of Bactria, but was to recover and expand very soon. When Artabanus I died, perhaps around 191 BC, Priapatius became king and ruled for fifteen years, leaving two sons, Mithradates and Phraates. The elder, Phraates, succeeded, and re-opened serious campaigning. Antiochus III had recently suffered a disastrous defeat in an encounter with the forces of the expanding Roman Republic at Magnesia, and was now too weak to defend his possessions. Phraates attacked the Mardi and other peoples of the Elburz range, and retook Hyrcania and other territories, pushing the Parthian boundary west of the Caspian Gates and settling some of the conquered population in the town of Charax near the Gates. But the full effects of Antiochus' defeat took some years to become apparent. First, the two kingdoms of Armenia revolted from Seleucid rule, followed by Media Atropatene. The death of Antiochus III and the inactivity of his successor provoked a whole chain of rebellions. One by one, the provinces of Iran were lost to the Seleucids, and became a series of independent monarchies. In the middle of this fragmentation of Iran, Phraates I of Parthia died, leaving the kingdom not to one of his many sons, but to his beloved younger brother Mithradates.

Plate 6a, aa

The astonishing military talents of Mithradates, usually regarded as the true founder of the Parthian Empire, were combined with a prudence that restrained their expression until

Plate 1

after the death of Antiochus IV Epiphanes in 163 BC. To the east, the Greek Demetrius had conquered the Punjab and ruled over Afghan and Indian terrain. Bactria fell into the hands of Eucratides. These two rulers fought so bitterly, that

Eucratides' resources were too much exhausted for him to prevent Mithradates from seizing Tapiura and Traxiane soon after 160 BC. The troubles of Eucratides were ended shortly afterwards. He was murdered by his son, who ran his chariot over his father's corpse and refused to allow its burial. A little later these Hellenic states of the Kabul valley and the Indus were united into a considerable empire, where the famous king Menander (the Milinda of the Indians) was to rule (*c.* 155–130 BC?). Having made conquests in India, he adopted Buddhism, and was remembered in Buddhist tradition.

Along the western route Mithradates advanced steadily. Media, the realm of a rebel king, Timarchus, was probably fully occupied by 148/7 BC, and one Bacasis was made governor. But the conqueror's attention seems then to have been diverted eastwards again, perhaps on account of an attack on his borders. From references which tend towards the romantic in classical authors, he probably campaigned in Arachosia and conquered territories up to the borders of India. While occupied with these conquests, Mithradates also issued the first coinage of the Parthians, an action which may have signified a complete and final break with Seleucid authority.

Plate 6a, aa

Towards the west Mithradates was now poised above the alluvial plains of Mesopotamia and Babylonia, dotted with cities, some of them already thousands of years old, which drew their wealth from the dual sources of agriculture and trade. The accession of the adolescent Demetrius II to the Seleucid throne and his subsequent involvement in fighting with a usurper, Tryphon, gave Mithradates the opportunity he needed. By July, 141 BC, he had annexed much of Babylonia and Mesopotamia in a swift campaign and had entered Seleucia on the Tigris itself. The consternation of Demetrius and the Babylonians at Mithradates' sudden appearance on the scene is reflected in contemporary clay records of Babylonia. But Mithradates' stay in Babylonia was short. He had to hasten eastwards to crush a

Bactrian invasion. At the same time Demetrius counter-attacked vigorously in Babylonia, assisted particularly by Greek elements there and in western Iran that were loyal to his dynasty.
An interesting theory proposes that collusion between Demetrius and Heliocles of Bactria produced these simultaneous attacks. But Mithradates crushed the Bactrians, and then returned
to defeat Demetrius. He captured the Seleucid king alive by a
trick and sent him off to an honourable retirement in Hyrcania,
giving him his own daughter Rhodogune in marriage. He then
confirmed the Parthian hold on central Iran and the Land of the
Plate 6b, bb Two Rivers. From Seleucia, he issued a fine and dated coinage,
using Demetrius' own die-cutters to produce it. By 140/39 BC,
as coins indicate, he was also master of Elymais and of Persis,
which remained a Parthian vassal province for centuries.

When Mithradates died peacefully about 138 BC, he had
transformed Parthia from a petty state in one corner of Iran into
a world empire, stretching from Babylonia to eastern Bactria.
He had issued the first Parthian coinage, on the Greek model,
and on these coins he justifiably calls himself 'great king'. He is
alleged to have attempted the codification of Iranian Law, and
the apparent re-naming of Nisa as Mithradatkirt probably took
place during his reign. It is no wonder that Arrian allots praise
(probably) to him in phrases similar to those he used of Alexander the Great. But the extension of the Parthian Empire was to
bring further conflict. When the young Phraates II succeeded
his father, his mother became regent. Demetrius attempted
twice to escape from his comfortable captivity in Hyrcania.
Each time he was recaptured and returned, the first time with a
severe reprimand from Phraates and the second with the insult-
ing gift of a pair of golden dice as a fitting reward for his child-
ish activities. In 130 BC, Phraates' kingdom was attacked
simultaneously from west and east. Antiochus VII Sidetes,
having disposed of the pretender Tryphon and consolidated
Judaea and Syria, set out to recover more territory. The size of

his army became almost legendary as did its luxurious appointment: cooks, bakers and actors abounded. In three battles,
Antiochus defeated the Parthian generals and recovered Babylonia and then Media. A number of Parthian subject territories
joined him, and he demanded impossible peace terms of
Phraates. But winter was approaching, and proved his undo-
ing. He quartered his men in and around Ecbatana. They behaved so badly that the populations turned against him. In
spring, a combination of the release of the captive Demetrius to
divide Seleucid loyalties, the simultaneous attack on the Seleucid army by the outraged populations of Media, and the ju-
dicious timing of Phraates' own counter-attack produced the
defeat and death of Antiochus. His body was sent to Syria in a
silver casket, his son Seleucus was made prisoner and his niece
was taken by Phraates into his harem. The royal favourite Himerus was made governor of Babylonia. This was the last serious attempt by a Seleucid monarch to recover Iran.

But events on the eastern frontier were still more threatening
to the Parthian state. In the earlier second century BC an attack
by the Hsiung-nu (Huns?) upon the Yueh-chih who inhabited
the north-west Chinese province of Kansu set in motion the
nomad tribes of central Asia. About 160 BC the Yueh-chih,
probably the Tochari of Western sources, in turn forced the Sak
tribes, the Saca nomads, westwards towards Ta-hsia (Bactria).
The main bulk of the invaders, mostly Sacaraucae and Massagetae, struck at north-eastern Parthia about 130 BC. The Greek
kingdom of Bactria disappeared under the nomad onslaught *c.*
120–100 BC, and the surviving petty Greek states of north-west
India were submerged under Saca extension by *c.* 50 BC. The
province of Parthia suffered also. During the fighting of about
128 BC, Phraates' captive Greek mercenaries suddenly turned
against him and in the subsequent massacre Phraates himself
was killed. Worse was to follow. When Phraates' (great-?) un-
cle Artabanus II had succeeded to the throne, the nomads who

took the western route overran the provinces of Parthia and Hyrcania, while others turned south-east to found the kingdom of Sacastene (Seistan). Artabanus too was killed fighting in the east about 124 BC. At the same time the Arab prince Hyspao-sines extended his kingdom of Mesene (or Characene) at the head of the Persian Gulf to include much of Babylonia, turn-ing the misdeeds of the Parthian governor Himerus to his own profit.

Parthian fortunes were therefore at a low ebb when Mithra-dates II, son of Artabanus, became king around 124/3 BC. But he rapidly showed himself a worthy possessor of the name of the 'great king'. First he retook Babylonia, and overstruck bronze coins of Hyspaosines (dated 121/0 BC) as a grim pub-lication of this success. He also attacked king Artavasdes of Armenia and took his son Tigranes prisoner. This was the first emergence into Parthian history of the Armenian state. The Parthians overran Mesopotamia and by 113 BC had entered Dura Europos. But Mithradates' greatest successes lay in the east. He recovered the provinces of Parthia and Aria, and made Saca stene (Seistan) at least nominally a vassal kingdom. Chin-ese reports based largely upon information gathered by the ambassador Ch'ang Ch'ien, who had himself visited Bactria *c.* 129 BC, credit Mithradates with sovereignty over the steppes east of the Caspian, including the oasis of Merv and the Mas-sagetae tribesmen. Mithradates had earned the period of peace in the east that accompanied the latter part of his reign.

There are indications of widespread administrative reorgan-isation during his period of rule. A geographical survey was produced, which was later utilised by Isidorus of Charax. A rock relief carved between 123 and 110 BC at Behistun/Bisutun in western Iran shows Mithradates facing four other figures. A Greek inscription identifies these as Gotarzes, satrap of satraps, Mithrates, Kophasates and another, probably also satraps. The relief presumably records the grant of power or fiefs to these

Fig. 4

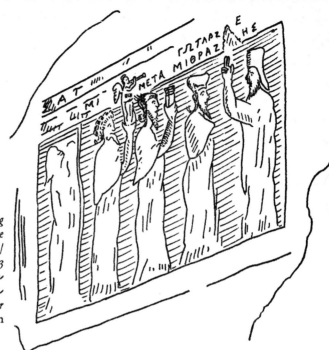

Fig. 4 Rock relief showing king Mithradates II before four of his vassals, Bebistun/Bisutun, carved between 123 and 110 BC and largely destroyed in the eighteenth century. Figures life-size. (After E. Herzfeld, Am Tor von Asien, fig. 11)

nobles. Its position beneath the bas-relief of the triumph of Darius I the Achaemenid can hardly have been accidental. The appearance of the Achaemenid title 'King of kings' for the first time in Parthian history on Mithradates' coins, and the publication of the claim that the Arsacid line was descended from Artaxerxes II Mnemon (a claim which seemingly replaced an earlier one of descent from the Seleucid satrap of Parthia) all reveal an attempt, politically motivated, to relate the Arsacid and Achaemenid dynasties. Mithradates' prestige was enhanced still further by the arrival of a Chinese embassy sent by the Han Emperor Wu-ti, and when these ambassadors returned Parthian envoys went with them carrying presents of 'ostrich eggs and clever Hyrcanian conjurers'. The trade route to the east known as the great Silk Route was now open.

Plate 6 c

Fig. 5 Denarius with the head of Sulla struck by Q. Pompeius Rufus c. 59 BC. About 3:1.

About 94 BC, Mithradates again became involved in western politics. The Armenian monarch died, and Mithradates placed the hostage Tigranes on the throne, receiving seventy valleys in payment. Then the Parthians invaded Mesopotamia, annexing the petty kingdoms of Adiabene, Gordyene and Osroene and making the Euphrates their western frontier. But a new power was approaching from the opposite direction. In 92 BC, the Roman general Sulla also reached the Euphrates. Mithradates sent an ambassador, Orobazus, to ask for an offensive and de-fensive alliance with Rome. Sulla clearly had no conception of the power or extent of Parthia, for he treated Orobazus with some contempt. A treaty or agreement was made, but the un-fortunate envoy was later executed for his failure to maintain Parthian prestige. For Parthia was now indubitably a power of world standing. Mithradates' embassies to Sulla and Wu-ti provided a link between Rome and China.

Mithradates' last years were clouded by rebellion. Tablets from Babylon dated *c.* 90 BC and after suddenly begin to name a king Gotarzes. Parthian documents under normal circum-stances mention the reigning monarch only by his title Arsaces. Mithradates' Satrap of satraps must have seized Babylonia as an independent ruler, and his personal name is given to distin-guish him from the other, and rightful, Arsaces. Mithradates

Fig. 5

did not recover this territory. His attention was diverted in 88 BC to a further outbreak of fraternal strife in the Seleucid family, and he received the unsuccessful Demetrius as hostage. The last coins of Demetrius are dated 88/7 BC, and it was probably in 87 that the King of kings died. His death was the signal for further troubles. Tigranes of Armenia immediately attacked Parthia, seized northern Mesopotamia and usurped the title 'King of kings'. Gotarzes I, now perhaps the ruling Arsaces, was supplanted in Babylonia by Orodes (I), and soon disappeared when the Sacarauca tribesmen interfered in Parthian affairs. They placed on the throne the aged Sinatruces. He refused to help Mithradates VI of Pontus in his struggle against Rome when an appeal came in 73 BC, and he died about 70. His son Phraates III succeeded to a kingdom depleted in size. The Parthian overlordship of the Massagetae of the Caspian steppes was gone. Worse, Sacastene and Arachosia had been lost, and formed into an independent Indo-Scythian kingdom. The most significant events of Phraates' reign, however, occurred not is this arena but on the western borders of the Empire. There, the final disintegration of the last remnants of the Seleucid realm was taking place, and new questions of international politics were being posed by the arrival of Rome.

CHAPTER III

Parthia and Rome

RELATIONS BETWEEN PARTHIA AND ROME were unfortunately to become all too frequently hostile. Territorial disputes were largely to blame. There were two main areas of enduring disagreement. The first was Armenia, and the second was the land between the Tigris and Euphrates rivers. Time and again these areas became the subject of bitter dissension and wasteful warfare. It is amazing to find the eastern Romans and the Persians still fighting for Armenia in the sixth century AD, six hundred years after the first clashes. Nevertheless it is to these encounters that we owe much information concerning Parthia, for such hostile contacts stimulated the attention of Roman writers. The periods and the works of peace were less interesting.

The Roman advance into Asia Minor and the resultant losses sustained by king Mithradates of Pontus and king Tigranes of Armenia soon involved the Parthians in active participation. At first Phraates III of Parthia was inclined to listen to the appeals of his fellow dynasts for help, but took no action. In 66 BC Pompey was appointed to replace Lucullus as Roman commander in Asia Minor, to continue operations against the kings of Pontus and Armenia. He hastened to secure Phraates' co-operation by promises of friendship and territory. But subsequently Pompey made a treaty with Tigranes of Armenia and handed over to him Gordyene, which had been promised to, and was indeed already occupied by, Phraates. The Parthians were expelled, and Phraates' protests were met with insults. The Parthians did not forget Pompey's trickery. Worse still, Pompey's lieutenant Gabinius ignored Phraates' wish that the Euphrates should be regarded as the Parthian frontier, and led a raiding expedition across it as far as the Tigris. Finally Pompey himself, like his predecessor, began to contemplate an invasion of Parthia. In 64 BC matters were settled for the time being: Phraates and Tigranes agreed to accept the arbitration of Pompey over boundaries, as they both recognised the need for union against the common enemy to the west.

About 58/7 BC Phraates III was murdered by his own sons, Mithradates and Orodes. They soon fell to fighting for the throne. Mithradates tried unsuccessfully to gain Roman assistance, but managed to seize Babylonia. Orodes II (called Hyrodes on his coins and by some authors) hounded down his brother, who gave himself up voluntarily in 55/4 BC. The treatment that he received was clearly unexpected. Orodes gave orders that Mithradates should be killed in his sight: the coins that he had minted in Seleucia were overstruck with a scene of Seleucia, personified, kneeling before Orodes. The latter was now undisputed king of the Parthians.

Plate 6d, dd

Plate 6e, ee

It was fortunate that this quarrel was now ended, for a new danger was threatening. In Rome, the Republican system of government was breaking down, and the aristocrats were competing for power. The political scene at this time was dominated by three powerful nobles who together formed a triumvirate, Caesar, Pompey and Crassus. The two last-named each held one of the two most important annual Roman magistracies, the consulships, for the year 55, after which Crassus was to hold the governorship of Syria – an appointment which he intended to use to make war on Parthia. Opposition at Rome was strong. There was no justification for an attack on Parthia. But the elderly Crassus, now over sixty years old, was led on by dreams of emulating the military glories of Caesar and Pompey. His victorious march into the east would surpass the success even of Alexander. What actually happened is vividly described in Plutarch's biography. During 55 Crassus recruited an army, using press-gangs where necessary, from the men unwanted by his two colleagues, and on the Ides of November set off from

Rome with his recruits. The attitude of the Roman crowds was menacing. In the gateway of the city sat the tribune Caius Ateius, leader of the opposition, with a brazier beside him, carrying out an ancient ritual to consign his opponent to the nether gods, a fitting opening to the ill-fated expedition. Undeterred, in April or May 54 Crassus arrived in Syria and took over the Syrian troops, so that his army now probably totalled seven legions, in all more than forty thousand men. He had little cavalry; he was relying on allies, the client kings of northern Mesopotamia and Armenia, to supply this. Among his officers Cassius, the future murderer of Caesar, was quaestor and his own son Publius Crassus was a legate.

The year 54 was passed in minor operations. Roman troops crossed the Euphrates a little way into Mesopotamia, scattered the scanty Parthian opposition and installed garrisons in some Greek towns. Orodes used the time to begin preparations for

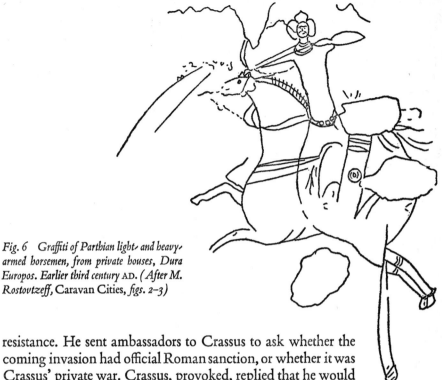

*Fig. 6 Graffiti of Parthian light- and heavy-
armed horsemen, from private houses, Dura
Europos. Earlier third century* AD. *(After M.
Rostovtzeff,* Caravan Cities, *figs. 2–3)*

resistance. He sent ambassadors to Crassus to ask whether the
coming invasion had official Roman sanction, or whether it was
Crassus' private war. Crassus, provoked, replied that he would
give his answer in Seleucia. At this the Parthian ambassador
held out his hand and said: 'Hair, Crassus, will grow on my
palm before you see Seleucia.'

As Crassus had left garrisons in several towns of northern
Mesopotamia, he would have to follow this route in attacking
Parthia. He therefore lost the cavalry and soldiers of king Artavasdes of Armenia, who had offered them on condition that
Parthia was entered through the hills of Armenia, where the
formidable Parthian cavalry would be least effective. In the
spring of 53 BC, Crassus crossed the Euphrates at Zeugma. As
his immediate objective was Seleucia on the Tigris, Cassius ad-
vised him to follow the Euphrates downstream. But a Roman
ally, king Abgar of Osroene, reported that Parthian forces were

Fig. 6

near by and were retreating eastwards across Mesopotamia. Crassus decided upon immediate pursuit. The Parthian army now emerges for the first time clearly into history. A cavalry force of some ten thousand men, commanded by Suren, a young noble of great talent from eastern Iran, was all that Orodes had ordered for the defence of Mesopotamia. He had led the Parthian infantry himself to Armenia, where he had expected Crassus to attack. Meanwhile Suren, followed by his cavalry, by a bodyguard of a thousand knights in mail armour and by numerous concubines, had been hovering in northern Mesopotamia. Crassus and his troops now struck out eastwards across a stretch of open country dotted with oases and settlements (described by the Roman writers as a trackless waste), in pursuit of the allegedly retreating Suren. On May 6 they reached the river Balicha (Balikh) below the town of Carrhae (Harran). The troops were tired and hungry after the march, and the officers called for a rest. But Crassus insisted on continuing the pursuit, allowed his men only a quick meal in the ranks, and then turned southwards after the Parthians, whose tracks had been spotted on the ground. Suddenly Crassus' scouts rode up to announce that the Parthians were on them. Immediately the remaining allied kings deserted with their horsemen, leaving the Romans dangerously short of cavalry. Crassus gave the order for all his troops to form up in an enormous square. The manoeuvre had been only partially completed when the attack began. The Parthians rode into sight over the rising ground. To the roar of kettledrums the mailed lancers charged, driving the Roman light-armed troops back on to the square. The heavy cavalry then retired, opening the way for the second, and still deadlier, section of the cavalry – the light-armed archers. The Romans were surrounded, and the hail of arrows began. The Parthian bows had a longer range than the Roman, and their arrows a more powerful impact, sufficient to penetrate Roman armour. The legionaries began to fall. If they made a sortie to drive back the Parthians, the mounted archers simply retired, shooting back as they retreated – the Parthian shot. The soldiers could achieve nothing, and were driven back to the square. But as yet the Romans were not seriously concerned. They expected that as soon as the archers' quivers were empty, their chance would come – until they saw Suren's camel trains laden with reserve supplies of arrows. Morale began to sink. Crassus' cavalry was not sufficient to attack the camels. Moreover, the square was not even fully formed yet, and the enemy, although outnumbered by more than three to one, was threatening the Roman flank. Publius was ordered to charge so as to give Crassus a moment of respite in which to complete the square. With his thirteen hundred cavalry, five hundred archers and four thousand soldiers, Crassus' son drove many of the Parthians before him. He and his men disappeared into a cloud of dust, cheering loudly. Crassus was given time to complete the formation, but at a cost. Publius quickly found that he had been lured into a trap. Once away from the main army, the the Parthians surrounded his force and rode around it pouring arrows into the throng. The soldiers retreated to a hillock. An urgent message for help reached Crassus. But he had no sooner started to move his forces than the 'fugitive' Parthians rode back bearing Publius' head impaled on the point of a lance. Only five hundred prisoners had been taken, and the officers were not among them.

The sight of Publius' head did nothing to restore Roman morale. Crassus behaved with courage and dignity in this crisis. He went up and down the ranks of soldiers saying that the loss was his alone, and that they must continue to fight for Rome. But to fight was impossible under the hail of arrows. Only nightfall brought a respite from the wounds and losses. Nightfall, however, brought no comfort to Crassus. He gave himself up so completely to despair, that his officers had to give the signal for retreat on their own authority. The silence in which this was intended to take place was broken by the cries of the four thousand wounded who were being left behind, and this noise must have indicated what was happening to the Parthians encamped near by. But they were not equipped for a night attack. By dawn, Crassus and most of the other Roman survivors were within the walls of near-by Carrhae. The Parthians slaughtered the Roman stragglers and wounded, and then surrounded the town. Neither provisions nor reinforcements were available to Crassus: retreat to the neighbouring hills was an urgent necessity. The Romans set out at night, but their guide treacherously delayed and misled them. Crassus' officer Octavius marched on ahead to safety with five thousand men: Cassius fled with some cavalry to Syria. Next day Suren surrounded Crassus' men, and, wishing to take him alive, proposed a meeting to discuss terms and safe conduct. Crassus saw through this offer, and hesitated to move until his men began to shout and abuse him. Then, courageously, he walked forward alone to meet his fate. Octavius, meanwhile, had returned to Crassus' aid, and with some officers followed him down. Suren offered Crassus a horse to go down to the Euphrates, where the treaty could be put in writing: 'for you Romans, at least, are not very good at remembering agreements' – a bitter reminder of Pompey's trickery. Crassus mounted, but Octavius, sensing treachery, seized the bridle. A scuffle ensued, and Crassus and his escort were killed. Of the rest of the Roman troops, many were taken prisoner, while others were hunted down by the Arabs. Suren allegedly gave a mock Roman triumph in Seleucia. Crassus' head and hand, so the story goes, were cut off and sent to Orodes in Armenia. Orodes and Artavasdes of Armenia were celebrating a political betrothal between their children with banquets and recitations from Greek literature. The actor Jason was reciting from Euripides' *Bacchae,* and when Crassus' head was brought in, to shouts of joy he seized it and sang the frenzied verses uttered by Agave over the head of

Pentheus. 'With such a farce, they say, the expedition of Crassus ended, like a tragedy.'

A tragedy indeed it was for Rome. Out of an army of more
than forty thousand men, a mere ten thousand had escaped to
Syria; ten thousand more were prisoners of the Parthians. The
rest were dead. The military standards of the Romans, the eagles,
were now in Parthian hands. The prisoners were marched off
to Merv, at the other extreme of the Parthian Empire, and settled
there. Unrest and rebellious feeling swept through the Jews
of the eastern Roman territories, who had long been in friendly
contact with the Parthians, and revolts had to be suppressed.
The campaign of Crassus went down in Roman annals as one
of the great disasters of Roman history. The might of Parthia
had been proved to the world; the Euphrates was henceforth
accepted as the frontier with Rome for more than a century.

But none of Crassus' chief opponents was to meet with a
fate much happier than his. Suren was the first to die, treacherously murdered on the orders of Orodes, who feared so talent-
ed a subject. In 51 BC the Parthians tardily followed up their
victory with an invasion of Syria under prince Pacorus, but this
was little more than a large-scale cavalry raid, resisted notably
by Cassius and Cicero. Pacorus was shortly recalled, as his activities became suspect to his father Orodes, and by 50 BC the
Parthians had withdrawn across the Euphrates. Nevertheless
the Parthians did not cease to interfere in Roman politics. It
was clearly in their interests to further the civil war developing
among the Romans, for their own protection and for possible
gains in territory. Orodes, therefore, was in communication
with Pompey before the latter's defeat and death, and Caesar
planned a great eastern campaign to put paid to Parthian interference. The assassination of Caesar saved the Parthians from
this threat, and thereafter they played a minor part in the ensuing civil war. In 40/39 BC, prince Pacorus, now reinstated in his
father's favour, and Labienus, a renegade Roman commander,

distinguished themselves in expeditions to Syria and Asia Minor, and seized both areas. In Palestine the Parthians were welcomed and assisted by a party among the Jews. But by 38 the tide had turned. Labienus had been killed; the Parthians were expelled from Syria, and Pacorus perished in the fighting.

Orodes, according to Justin, was so deeply distressed by the loss of the brilliant Pacorus that his mind became unbalanced. About 37 BC he decided to hand over the government to one of his thirty sons. His choice of the eldest, Phraates (IV), was unhappy. To secure his position, Phraates murdered first his father and then all his brothers. When his savagery began subsequently to be directed against the nobility, numbers of them fled the kingdom. Among the latter was a noble named Monaeses, who went to the Romans. He persuaded Mark Antony that he could direct the Roman army in Parthia, and that the Parthians as a whole were ready to rise against Phraates. Attracted by the prospect of easy conquest, Antony prepared for invasion. King Artavasdes of Armenia was forced to become a Roman ally and to provide cavalry. In spring, 36 BC, Antony crossed the Euphrates at Zeugma, and following Artavasdes' advice led his army, which now totalled about one hundred thousand men, into Media Atropatene. In order to advance more quickly, he divided his forces. Two legions under Statianus were assigned to guard the slower-moving baggage train, with the precious siege-engines in it, which was to follow behind the main force as quickly as it could. Antony hastened on to the capital of Media Atropatene, Praaspa. This he had to besiege; but as the siege engines had not yet arrived, he was forced to construct great mounds of earth to replace the customary siege-towers. Phraates, profiting by this separation, launched an attack on the baggage train. Some ten thousand soldiers or more were killed, the rest were taken captive, the baggage and engines were destroyed, and Artavasdes of Armenia once again deserted the Roman cause.

Plate 6f, ff

Antony was now in difficulties. His foraging parties were slaughtered, his men showed cowardice, and the Romans suffered continually from Parthian cavalry tactics and archery. At last, as winter was approaching and all attempts at negotiation had failed, Antony was forced to retreat. The miseries of the Romans grew. Antony followed the hills towards Armenia; his troops were harried constantly by the Parthians and suffered severely from hunger and thirst. Loaves of bread passed hands for silver only; the starving soldiers were reduced to drinking tainted water and scrabbling beneath stones for plants to chew as they went along. Many were dying from the effects of this diet. A friendly Parthian warned Antony that the fate of Crassus awaited his troops if ever they left the hills. The retreat dragged on with increasing losses and demoralisation. At last they reached a river not far from the borders of Armenia. Here the Parthians ceased their attack, unstrung their bows and rode off praising the courage and endurance of the Romans. After six more days, and nearly a month since they had left Praaspa, the Romans reached Armenia. Antony reviewed his troops; fighting and disease had wiped out thirty-five thousand of his men. Although no battle had actually resulted in defeat, one third of his army was dead, and in numbers of men killed Antony's losses far exceeded those of Crassus. Even yet the Romans were not safe; Antony had to treat the shifty Artavasdes in a friendly fashion so as to gain the supplies desperately needed for his men. Eight thousand men more were lost in the march to Syria through the onset of harsh weather. Antony spent the winter in Egypt, recuperating at Alexandria in the company of Cleopatra.

This was the first, and it was to prove the last serious invasion by the Romans of the highlands of Iran. Phraates IV, to make public his success, overstruck with his own types the coins of Antony found in the Roman baggage train. Antony subsequently recovered Armenia for a short while, and in 33 BC marched to the borders of Media. But as soon as he withdrew the Parthians and Armenians regained their territories, and within three years he was dead. Phraates was shortly faced with further troubles. A usurper, Tiridates (II), had come out in open revolt by 31. Phraates had to take refuge with the 'Scythians', a generic term in antiquity for the nomad tribes to the north of Iran. With their help he chased Tiridates into Syria, but the latter managed to steal a son of Phraates as he fled to the Romans. This son was eventually returned on condition that Phraates restored the Roman standards captured at Carrhae. The Parthian king bided his time. In 26, Tiridates re-entered Mesopotamia with such speed that Phraates, before retreating, had to kill his politically valuable harem. Tiridates issued coins from the mints of Babylonia, some of which bore the legend 'Philo-romaeus', friend of Rome. By summer 25, however, he had been permanently expelled from Parthia. At last, in May, 20 BC, Phraates returned the Roman standards and many of the Roman prisoners taken during the campaigns of Crassus and Antony. To Augustus, first emperor of the Romans, and to his contemporaries this was a diplomatic success of the first

Fig. 7 importance, worthy of widespread public commemoration. Relations between Parthia and Rome were improved by this action. Augustus was able to stop pretending that he proposed to invade Parthia, and presented Phraates with an Italian slave girl named Musa for his harem. He presumably realised the practical difficulties of warfare in Parthia, and perhaps also the weakness of the Parthian monarchy.

Whether Augustus foresaw the amazing future career of Musa is impossible to say. By her, Phraates had a son, Phraates V, usually called Phraataces. From being a concubine, Musa became a queen. About 10 BC, she persuaded Phraates IV to send his four older sons and their families to Rome, where they could live as befitted their rank – and in safety. Perhaps this action was connected with the fleeting appearance of a usurper,

Fig. 7   Scene of the return, in 20 BC, of the Roman standards lost at Carrhae, from the breastplate of the statue of Augustus found at Prima Porta, Rome

Plate 6g

Mithradates, about this time. In any case, this meant that the way was clear in 2 BC for Musa to poison Phraates and to place her son Phraataces on the throne. Before 1 BC the Parthians and Armenians combined to eject a Roman nominee from the throne of Armenia and to substitute their candidate, Tigranes, and his sister-wife. This provoked Augustus to organise an expedition to restore order, which was put under the command of his grandson Gaius. Some think it was for Gaius' information that Isidorus of Charax compiled his *Parthian Stations*. Fortunately, Phraataces and Gaius were able to settle the matter amicably in the Roman favour at banquets held on either side of the Euphrates. A young Roman officer present at the occasions, Velleius Paterculus, later described Phraataces as a fine youth. In AD 2, Phraataces was married – to his mother Musa.

Plate 6gg

This act was doubtless no less political than the more celebrated union of Oedipus, but it filled the Greeks and Romans with horror. The heads of both Musa and her son-husband appeared on their coins. But in AD 4 Phraataces was either murdered or driven into exile and death, and nothing more is heard of the remarkable Musa. Their unpopular Arsacid successor, Orodes III, was assassinated within three years of his accession.

The rapidity with which Phraataces and Orodes III had lost their thrones – and lives – underlined the increasing weakness of the Parthian monarchy. These difficulties were not lessened by continual struggles over the Armenian throne. Both Parthians and Romans claimed that the strategically important kingdom of Armenia was within their sphere of influence. It was therefore a matter of great importance to both sides whether the king was a Parthian or Roman nominee. In an attempt to solve the problem firstly of the vacant Parthian throne, the Parthian nobility requested Augustus to send them one of the four sons of Phraates IV, and received the eldest as king Vonones I. But Vonones' western ways rapidly irritated the nobles. His dislike of the hunting and banqueting of aristocratic life, and his lack of interest in horses, soon resulted in the appearance of another candidate for the throne, the Arsacid king of Media Atropatene, Artabanus III. After an unsuccessful first attempt, Artabanus defeated Vonones in battle and was crowned about AD 12. During his long reign, he seems to have done much to restore the power of the central government. In AD 35, his throne was threatened by a plot to replace him by another son of Phraates IV, also named Phraates, who had then been living in Rome for nearly half a century. But Phraates got no further than Syria; there he died, either through a failure to adapt to the conditions of Near Eastern life, or through Artabanus' plotting. Nothing daunted, Tiberius, Augustus' successor, sent in a grandson of Phraates IV, Tiridates III. A campaign of bribery within Parthia itself was so effective that Artabanus had to flee and take refuge with the tribes east of the Caspian sea. Tiridates was welcomed by the Greek cities of west Parthia and was crowned at Seleucia; then he set siege to a fortress in which Artabanus' treasure and concubines were kept. But again the Romanised nominee proved unpopular. A group of nobles sought out Artabanus in Hyrcania and found him dressed in rags and living by his bow. In response to their

Plate 6i, ii

Plate 6ii

summons, he collected some Saca and Daha tribesmen, chased out Tiridates, and made a formal settlement with the Romans. Joy at Artabanus' return was not universal. About AD 35 the great commercial city of Seleucia had rebelled against Parthian authority (or rather the lack of it), and had declared itself independent unilaterally. This independence Seleucia now maintained in spite of Artabanus' return and siege operations by the Parthians. Matters were made no easier by an alleged temporary abdication of Artabanus in favour of one Cinnamus.

Upon Artabanus' death shortly afterwards, about AD 38, Gotarzes II seems to have succeeded. Like his predecessor he was probably not of direct Arsacid descent but from a collateral branch of the family, in his case connected with the noble Hyr-canian line of Gew. Some of his deeds appear in heroic form in the *Shahnameh*, a testimony to the troubled nature of his reign, few epics being concerned with peacetime. Gotarzes was rapid-ly chased into exile by his brother Vardanes, who continued the siege of Seleucia, basing himself probably upon Ctesiphon, once a garrison town and now a winter capital. Eventually, about AD 40, the two brothers divided the Empire between them, Vardanes taking the larger part, while Gotarzes re-tained Hyrcania and other northern provinces. In the midst of this complicated situation, during the spring of 42, the philo-sopher Apollonius of Tyana travelled through Mesopotamia and Babylonia on his way east to India. It is significant that he did not visit Seleucia, then still under siege. But in June 42 the city voluntarily surrendered to Vardanes, after seven years of independence. Soon afterwards the royal brothers quarrelled, and in the ensuing struggle Gotarzes was finally victorious. Vardanes was murdered while out hunting, probably in AD 47/8. Even so, Gotarzes found himself next year with another rival to combat. A party of nobles had summoned from Rome a further grandson of Phraates IV, Meherdates, and battle was inevitable. Gotarzes played for time, sacrificed on mount Sanbulos and was ultimately victorious. He spared his rival but had his ears shorn, so that, being imperfect in body, Meherdates could never rule again. To commemorate this victory Gotarzes had a rock relief cut at Behistun about AD 50. He appears on horseback lancing an enemy, and an inscription in Greek labels him as Gotarzes, son of Gew. Next year he was dead.

Plate 6j

Vonones II, successor to Gotarzes II, reigned but a few months, and was succeeded by Vologases I, the son of a Greek concubine. He sensibly gave his brother Pacorus the throne of Media, and another brother Tiridates the throne of Armenia, where Tiridates was eventually installed about AD 54. The latter action could not fail to provoke Roman intervention, as the Romans too had claims on Armenia. Accordingly, the advisers of the young Nero prepared for war. The seasoned general Corbulo was appointed to the task of recovering Armenia. He found the eastern Roman legions in a deplorable condition produced by decades of inactivity. He therefore set himself to train them into a usable army, and the soldiers suffered nearly as much from his training as from the ensuing campaign. Two summers of drilling were followed by a winter under canvas in part of Armenia. In the piercing cold, frost-bite crippled the men and sentries died at their posts from exposure. Deserters were executed. In spring 58, the campaign proper opened. Tiridates was unable to prevent Corbulo from taking his capital Artaxata and razing it. Vologases, distracted by internal revolts, the secession of Hyrcania and the activities of a usurper, (Vardanes II?), was unable to assist his brother. Next year Corbulo advanced on the other important city of Armenia, Tigranocerta. The inhabitants closed the gates against him. To dissuade them from holding out for long Corbulo executed a captive Armenian noble in his camp and fired the head into the town. It landed right in the middle of a council of war, and the town promptly surrendered. In AD 60, Tiridates counterattacked, but was easily driven out of the kingdom. Armenia

was now in Roman hands and a Roman nominee was placed
upon the throne; Corbulo retired to Syria. A new Parthian
offensive, however, caused the appointment of a further officer,
Paetus, to take command in the Armenian region while Corbulo defended Syria. Paetus invaded Armenia in 62. As winter approached, he regarded the campaigning season as over and
allowed many of his men to go on leave. A sudden strong
counter-attack by Vologases forced the incompetent Paetus to
capitulate: the Romans were to withdraw from Armenia.
Paetus himself led the retreat, marching forty miles a day and
abandoning the wounded. At last, in 63, a compromise was
reached. Tiridates was to receive the crown of Armenia, but
from the hands of Nero in Rome. Thus Roman honour and
Parthian claims were at once satisfied. Three years later Tiridates made the journey to Rome. As a Magus or priest he had
to observe the religious rules which forbade him to defile water,
and he travelled by land. At Rome, in ceremonies of the greatest
pomp, Nero placed the crown of Armenia on the head of Tiridates, and sent with him on his return squads of workmen to
rebuild the city of Artaxata.

The period of Vologases I, who reigned probably until AD
80, saw the rise to prominence of certain Oriental features in Parthian culture. For the first time, Aramaic lettering is used on the
royal coinage. A fire altar now appears among the designs of
the official coin issues. This public recognition of the worship
of fire gives credence to the Zoroastrian religious tradition
which attributed the collection of the surviving manuscripts
and traditions of the sacred book, the Avesta, to a king Valakhsh (Vologases), who may be Vologases I. Furthermore
Vologases founded a new city in Babylonia, Vologasias, placed
close to Seleucia for the obvious purpose of undermining the
powerful influence of the (originally) Greek city. Other cities,
such as Susa and Merv, were from this period known by their
native, no longer by their Seleucid Greek, names.

Plate 6j

For decades after Corbulo's campaigns, relations between Parthia and Rome remained more or less peaceful, and therefore the Roman authors have little to say of events in Parthia. The consolidation of the Roman frontiers that was taking place at this period under Vespasian meant that the Euphrates was confirmed as the western boundary of Parthia, and buffer states such as that of Palmyra were now drawn securely into the Roman orbit. About AD 72, the nomad horde of the Alani swept into Parthia from the north-east. The ruler of the now seemingly independent province of Hyrcania wisely made an alliance with them, and perhaps with his encouragement they poured on past his kingdom into northern Iran. In Media they seized the harem of the ruler Pacorus; in Armenia they routed the forces of King Tiridates and almost captured him by dexterous use of the lasso. Appeals to the Romans for help were of little avail, and it was fortunate for the Parthians that the Alani ultimately returned eastwards of their own accord, and laden with spoil.

Vologases I disappears from history about AD 80. In 77/8 both a Vologases (II?) and a king named Pacorus (II) were striking coins at Seleucia, and so internal strife must once again have broken out. Another Parthian pretender, Artabanus IV, struck coins at Seleucia in 80/1, but was shortly suppressed, apparently leaving Pacorus II sole ruler – but not for long. Some coins issued in 89/90 are now attributed to the second Vologases, and the numbering of these kings should probably be revised. The fleeting appearance of a pseudo-Nero, who was impersonating the recently dead Roman emperor, on the Euphrates in 79, and of another pseudo-Nero in 89, may indicate Parthian attempts to turn Roman political methods back upon themselves. The emperor Domitian contemplated an invasion of Parthia, as poets of his time indicate. But although assassination saved the Parthians from Domitian's plans, one of Domitian's officers was to fulfil a similar dream.

The internal situation in Parthia now becomes extremely complex. Coin issues adumbrate the struggles that must have been taking place. Pacorus II struck coins until AD 87, and then again in 92–96, and lastly from about 113 to 115. A king Osroes (called Chosroes on a coin), the brother of Pacorus II, issued coins sporadically between about 89/90 and 127/8. The issues of his rival Vologases (probably III) occur between about AD 105 and the late 140s. Mere glimpses of the period appear in written sources. Kan Ying arrived in Mesene from China in 97, and in 101 a king of Parthia named 'Man-ch'iu' sent gifts to China of lions and ostriches.

In AD 113, to add to Parthia's difficulties, a Roman emperor once again planned an eastern expedition. Several of his predecessors had been prepared to ignore the lessons of Carrhae and Praaspa, but had not proceeded beyond words. Trajan, long a soldier, was above all a man of action. Trajan's precise motives in attacking Parthia have been much discussed, but after all the argument Dio Cassius' reason still remains cogent and comprehensible: what led the emperor on was simply 'a passion for glory'. An immediate excuse for interference was provided by events in Armenia. The Parthian monarch Osroes had deposed the king of Armenia without the consent of Rome. Thus Osroes had broken the long-standing arrangements over the monarchy of Armenia. On news of Trajan's approach in 113, Osroes sent ambassadors to the emperor at Athens, requesting peace and an agreement to place on the disputed throne Parthamasiris, son of Pacorus. No answer was given. Next year, Trajan marched into Armenia with his troops, and encountered no opposition. Local kings hastened to meet him. At Elegia, he received Parthamasiris before the whole army. The prince took off the diadem that he had assumed and laid it at Trajan's feet, expecting the emperor to replace it, as Nero had done with Tiridates. Instead, Trajan announced publicly his intention to make Armenia a Roman province. The scene is shown on an issue of Roman bronze coins. Parthamasiris was escorted from the camp, and died mysteriously soon afterwards, many said by the orders of Trajan. Armenia was placed under a Roman governor. Then Trajan turned southwards, perhaps to test the allegiance of the local kings of northern Mesopotamia. Abgar VII of Edessa, only too well aware of the suspicion which surrounded his allegiance, sent to Trajan his handsome son, an emissary well calculated to win the emperor's favour. Other dynasts fled, leaving Trajan in occupation of Meso-potamia, which he also annexed as a Roman province. Con-solidation occupied the year 115. Well satisfied with these events, Trajan returned to Antioch for the winter of 115/6. While he was there, a tremendous earthquake struck the city and left a third of it in ruins. Trajan himself had a narrow escape, and had to camp out in the hippodrome.

Next year, Trajan revealed further ambitions. For how long he had contemplated his actions is not clear. One action may simply have led him to the next. In spring, AD 116, he crossed the Euphrates in specially constructed boats, conquered Adia-bene and left his subordinates to turn it into the Roman pro-vince of Assyria, while he went on to further glory. Ctesiphon, the Parthian capital, was now his aim. After a comparatively short resistance the city fell, and a daughter and the golden throne of Osroes were among Trajan's spoil. To complete the campaign for 116, Trajan marched down to Mesene and receiv-ed the submission of Attambelus V. Trajan's suzerainty there-fore now extended right over the trade routes of Mesopotamia and Babylonia, and over the thriving city of Spasinu Charax not far from the ports of the Persian Gulf. While there, Trajan stood on the shore of the Gulf and watched a ship set sail for India; wistfully, he regretted that his age prevented him from emulating Alexander further.

So far, Osroes had been unable to protect his possessions or to counter-attack because of internal struggles. But by mid 116

Fig. 8 Bronze sestertii issued by Trajan in commemoration of his military successes in the east. Approximately actual size.
(A) Reverse: Trajan, seated on a platform, extends his hand to the kneeling king Parthamasiris, as Roman soldiers look on. AD *114–5.* REX PARTHVS *S(ENATVS) C(ONSULTO). (B) Reverse: Trajan, seated on a platform, places a diadem on the head of king Parthamaspates. On the ground kneels a figure symbolising Parthia.* AD *116–7.* REX PARTHIS DATVS. S(ENATVS) C(ONSVLTO)

he was at least temporarily free to organise opposition. Parthian forces attacked Trajan's conquests at key positions, and some of the vassal kings, Abgar VII among them, broke out into revolt. Trajan himself heard of the rebellion at Babylon, where he had gone on a visit to pay homage in the room where Alexander died. Energetic action soon recovered Mesopotamia and most of Armenia, but Assyria was probably lost and Babylonia presented a problem. Trajan had to act quickly and decisively. He retained Mesopotamia and Armenia as provinces, but handed over Babylonia with Ctesiphon to a Parthian prince with Armenian connexions named Parthamaspates, who was to rule as client-king. While returning to Syria, Trajan turned aside to set siege to the rebel desert city of Hatra. Sun, thirst and innumerable flies drove the Romans back, although they managed to breach the walls, and Trajan retired to Antioch leaving Hatra in rebel hands. In the spring of 117, Trajan prepared to enter Mesopotamia again; but his health was

Fig. 8B

failing, and by early August he was dead. With far-sighted wisdom his successor Hadrian handed back the newly won territories to their rulers and to client kings. Armenia was left to a Parthian monarch; Parthamaspates, expelled from Ctesiphon, was compensated with Osroene, and Osroes' daughter was returned. For another half-century the Romans ceased active interference in the east, and the Parthians were left to pursue their dynastic struggles in peace.

CHAPTER IV

King and Government

THE PARTHIANS, as Tarn said, entered a ready-made kingdom. Coming from a nomad background, they made few immediate alterations in the complex Seleucid administration. The lack of official Parthian documents severely hampers the study of their institutions, for few Greek or Roman writers paid much attention to them. Indeed, the very name by which the Parthians called their realm is unknown. The Achaemenids knew themselves as Aryans. The successors of the Parthians in Iran, the Sasanians, called their empire Eranshahr, the kingdom of the Aryans; perhaps the Parthians did likewise. Greek sources suffer from a confusion of Aryans with Arianoi, the inhabitants of the eastern Iranian province of Aria.

The Parthians ruled their kingdom for nearly half a millennium, and enormous changes clearly took place during that time. At first, the Seleucid territorial divisions were maintained, based as they were on the great Achaemenid provinces, the satrapies. These the Seleucids subdivided into eparchies, hyparchies and the fortified village, or *stathmos*. But there was a strong tendency for the great satrapies to be broken up into smaller eparchies, which became the basic administrative divisions by the first century BC. Appian, writing in the second century AD, speaks of seventy-two 'satrapies', by which he meant these eparchies. But there were kingdoms as well as satrapies within the Empire. Pliny mentions the existence of eighteen in his day (the later first century AD), eleven 'upper' and seven 'lower' kingdoms. These substates included the important kingdoms of Greater Media, with its cities Ecbatana and Rhagae, and Media Atropatene, with Ga(n)zaca and the capital Praaspa. Armenia was long a sphere of Parthian influence, and finally fell into Arsacid hands in the 50s AD, after which

Fig. 1

Arsacids held it for centuries. The primary capital of Armenia lay at Artaxata. The area around the western Parthian frontier was dotted with smaller kingdoms after the Seleucid collapse, many of them equivalent in extent to Seleucid eparchies. That of Adiabene was ruled in the earlier first century AD by kings called Izates, and it included the town Arbela, where the later Parthian monarchs were allegedly buried. Osroene was ruled from Edessa by a line of Arab kings named Abgar; Arabs again ruled the kingdom of Hatra in northern Mesopotamia. Among those who rose against the last ruler of the Parthians was a king Domitian of Kirkuk. Round the head of the Persian Gulf stretched the kingdom of Mesene or Characene, where kings with names of mixed origin held the vital sea-ports below Spasinu Charax. Eastward lay the kingdoms of Elymais and Persis; in the latter, there were local princes who seemingly regarded themselves as the successors of the Achaemenids. Conditions elsewhere in the Empire are almost unknown, as they were further from the ken of western writers. Hyrcania may possibly have become an independent kingdom for a time, for Hyrcanian ambassadors reached Rome in the first century AD, but no coinage was issued, and there are no coins to clarify the situation in eastern Iran either. Numerous petty kingdoms, ruled by local chieftains, must have existed in the more remote and inaccessible parts of the realm, and nomad tribes wandered as they do today.

Plate 6n

The cities of the Empire were placed under Parthian governors. Greek towns and military colonies previously 'free' usually retained a local autonomy and their characteristic constitutions and laws. Magistrates continued to be elected by the citizens and the city councils still functioned, as is testified at Susa and Seleucia. The Council and Assembly of Susa passed decrees: magistrates there were proposed by the Council, but could not stand for election until their qualifications had been scrutinised; this done, the people could elect their magistrates

Fig. 9 Graffito showing a Parthian king, Dura Europos. Second or early third century AD. *(After M. Rostovtzeff,* Caravan Cities, *fig. 1)*

from the Council's candidates. The power and position of these towns remained great until the early first century AD after which they began to decline.

The precise relationships between these various subdivisions of the Empire and the central government are far from clear and probably altered often, as the amount of control exercised over the local rulers and governors varied. But a general trend towards increased decentralisation and local independence can be observed in the last two centuries of Parthian rule.

The Parthian king occupied a position which at first closely resembled that of many of the Hellenistic Greek monarchs. Likewise owner and absolute ruler of his Empire, he was surrounded by Bodyguards and Honoured Friends on the

Fig. 9

Plate 6

Hellenistic model. Familiar Seleucid titles appear on his coins: Saviour, Benefactor, Victor and others. Family and kinship were of vital importance to the crown. Only to the Arsacid family did the aristocracy show loyalty and obedience. Any male of Arsacid lineage, from whatever branch of the family, provided that he was physically unblemished, would be acceptable as monarch. Only the question as to which individual Arsacid was to rule could be – and often was – a matter for dispute. The rulers strengthened their position by the manipulation of family connexions in several ways. In the first place they seem to have enhanced the prestige of their own line by adopting as their ancestor, through propaganda, first perhaps the Seleucid satrap of Parthia and later the Achaemenid monarch Artaxerxes II Mnemon. Secondly, we hear of the appointment of members of the Arsacid family to some of the subordinate thrones within the Empire – to the kingdoms of Media and Armenia for instance. Furthermore, the importance attached to the royal harem was no mere *grotesquerie* of Oriental life or testimony to monarchical depravity. Almost every concubine was a princess, the daughter of a vassal king or noble, or was at least, like Musa, a friendly gift from another potentate. Thus nearly every member of the harem represented a dynastic alliance or pledge of friendship, and the group an essential network of political connexions. At the head of the harem stood the queen or queens. These could include the king's sisters, as we learn from parchments found at Avroman in Kurdistan, and on at least one occasion his mother. Although little is said of the activities or influence of the queens in the ancient sources, they may well have had as much effect behind the scenes as any queen of Egypt or Roman empress. Names of the queens were sometimes coupled with that of the monarch in the dating of documents. When necessary a queen could act as regent, and the astonishing career of the ex-slave girl Musa shows what a really determined woman could achieve.

Plate 5

Arrangements over the succession upon the death of a mon-arch are obscure, but must have allowed room for disagreement. This constituted one of the weaknesses of the Arsacid state, as the frequent dynastic struggles testify. Justin tells us that nor-mally the king was succeeded by his eldest son, but that some-times a brother might succeed, as when Mithradates I followed Phraates I. Other cases of brother succession occurred later, and it seems to have been one of the nomad customs that survived in Parthian society. Strabo adds that the kings were appointed from the two Councils of the Parthian state, one of Kinsmen (of the monarch, a title simply indicating 'nobles') and the sec-ond of Wise Men and Magi, but he does not explain how.

The Parthian nobility, like the Achaemenian, allegedly com-prised seven great families, and a number of middle and lesser clans. The figure seven is disputable, but the family names, principal domains and political activities of several of the great houses can be distinguished. The Behistun rock relief of Mithradates II may show him granting fiefs to four heads of these houses. The Suren family was based on Seistan, and had the hereditary right to crown the king at the coronation ceremony. When kings of mainstream Arsacid descent were replaced by the less direct line of Artabanus III, an Arsacid by his moth-er only, the Suren clan continued to support rivals of more purely Arsacid descent. The most famous exploit of this family was of course the defeat of Crassus in 53 BC. The house of Karen, whose seat lay probably at Nihavand in Media, also on occasion opposed the ruling monarch. The family of Gew was based on Hyrcania, and of Mihran on Rhagae. These 'feudal' princes, rulers in their own domains, had courts on the royal model; it was the custom, says Strabo, for the kings of Media to have many wives – that is, the usual royal harem. Suren took his harem with him on his campaign against Crassus, a public demonstration of his political importance. Plutarch describes the ten thousand cavalrymen of Suren at Carrhae as his depend-

Fig. 4

ants and slaves, that is, his subjects from Seistan who formed his army, and presumably the other princes maintained similar forces of their own. Only a strong Arsaces could enforce allegiance upon such a nobility.

The study of the Parthian administration and of the offices of the bureaucracy is made extremely difficult by the scarcity and the obscurity of the surviving evidence. This consists of scattered inscriptions and documents, the majority of which were found at Dura Europos, Nisa and Susa. Greek and Roman writers mention Parthian officials; not only do they use terms loosely, however, but their terms are often difficult to equate with Iranian offices. Ranks and titles seem to have varied widely across the realm, and the three categories of Iranian name – the title, the honorific and the personal name – are not always easy to distinguish. Titles and protocol became elaborately developed. The variation in titulary throughout the Empire, however, indicates the lack of a strong, centralised and unified organisation such as that forged by the Romans. Consequently it is impossible as yet to give any clear account of Parthian offices. Presumably the leading body of state was Strabo's Council of Kinsmen or nobles, called the Senate by Justin. This would have been attended by the vassal princes and the heads of the great families. Doubtless it gained in importance as the power of the monarchy declined in the later Parthian period. But we hear of neither this Council nor the second Council of Wise Men and Magi in Parthian political history.

Among the senior officials of the realm was the *marzban* or governor-general, who in the Nisa documents is set above the satrap. The highest titles included the Bodyguards, Friends and Sceptre-holders, dignitaries known from the Achaemenian and Seleucid Empires. An important parchment contract in Greek from Dura, dated AD 121, mentions further high officials. Manesus, the son of Phraates, was 'one of the *batesa* and of the Freemen, collector of taxes and *strategos* of Mesopotamia and

Parapotamia, and *Arabarch*'. The sheer number of Manesus' posts is striking, and was probably a common feature of Parthian administration. The term *batesa*, doubtless a rank, appears in many forms in north-west Iran, in Armenia and at Hatra, and must mean 'lord' or the like. The rank of the Freemen, a translation of the Iranian term *azatan*, was also a high one. *Strategos*, a surviving Seleucid term for governor, and *Arabarch*, ruler of the Arabs or desert police officer, pose fewer problems. Subordinate to Manesus was Phraates the eunuch, *arkapates* – another high rank or office. The post of satrap, a provincial governor in the Achaemenid era, lost much of its old importance in Parthian times. The title Satrap of satraps appears in the Greek inscription above the rock relief of Mithradates II at Behistun, where the office still seems to have been significant. Thereafter in Parthian documents it designates such posts as that of city-governor only, like Khwasak, satrap of Susa in AD 215. Zamaspes is called both satrap and *stratiarch* (an equivalent, used for purposes of metre, of *strategos*), of Susa in a Greek verse inscription of AD 1/2. Western writers continued to use the term loosely of many offices. Below the satrap were minor officials, such as the *dyzpty* at Nisa, the head of a fortified village. Royal, and not private, seals were used by these officials for validating documents.

Eunuchs featured fairly prominently in the administration. Apollonius of Tyana encountered them on his journey across Parthia. Tacitus knew that they could hold office, and they did so in both civil and military spheres. Furthermore, it is not generally realised that inhabitants of Roman Syria also sometimes became officials in western Parthia. Between AD 130 and 140, Iarhai of Palmyra was the satrap of Thilwana, a locality in the sub-kingdom of Meherdates, prince of Mesene; A'abei the Palmyrene was a magistrate, or *archon*, in the same area; and Soados the son of Boliades held a position in Vologasias. The Parthian military hierarchy included posts of some importance, although of course the standing army was small. We hear of

Fig. 4

Plate 73

commanders of garrisons, at Dura for instance. Philostratus' description of the head of the garrison at Babylon as a 'satrap' does not help to clarify Parthian terminology.

For what it is worth, Moses of Chorene gives a sketch of the Armenian state as organised on Parthian lines by the Arsacid ruler Tiridates shortly after AD 60. Posts around the royal person, and the important positions of master of the royal hunts, chamberlain, head of sacrifices, falconer, guardian of the summer residences and so on were distributed among the members of the great families. Fiefs were granted to Tiridates' vassals and four territorial Wardens of the Marches were appointed, one to the region at each cardinal point of the compass. The army was divided into the permanent frontier garrisons and the 'feudal' levies summoned only at time of war. Local justices were appointed for town and country, and times for royal audiences, consultations and entertainments were fixed. Perhaps a grain of truth underlies Moses' account; a prince of Hatra between AD 130 and 140 indeed held an honorific title 'master of hunting'. Altogether, the fusion discernible in the Parthian state between the 'feudal' Iranian and the urban Seleucid organisations is remarkable.

The great trilingual inscription of the Sasanian monarch Shapur I (*c.* AD 240–72) on the so-called Ka'bah of Zoroaster at Naqsh-i Rustam lists the most prominent members of the court of Ardashir, the first Sasanian ruler, in order of importance. First come four kings of eastern Iran (of the Parthian region, of Merv, Seistan and Kerman); then three queens, Ardashir the *bitaxsh* and a high official named Papak – all probably members of the ruling family. Next in importance are mentioned the heads of the noble families of Iran, the chiefs of the scribes and of the armoury, and finally other officials and persons of rank. This order was doubtless inherited from the time of the last Parthian rulers. The lack of a centralised royal bureaucracy is striking; 'feudalism' is now dominant.

The Parthian army seems to have been similarly lacking in a strong central command. In central Asia the Parni were used to conditions where numerous horse-archers predominated and mounted mail-clad tribal aristocrats alone fought at close quarters. In Iran they found, and probably at first partly adopted, Seleucid tactics, for which mercenary forces, consisting of light- and heavy-armed infantry and of cavalry, were employed. Mithradates I must have owed much of his success to such forces. But in the fighting against the Sacas around 130 BC, king Phraates II encountered serious trouble with his mercenaries; not long afterwards, perhaps in the time of Mithradates II, Parthian tactics underwent a revolution. The formations and the armament of the Seleucids were abandoned almost entirely. Mercenaries were untrustworthy: Seleucid cavalry could not break a line of heavy-armed spearmen, and horse-archers frequently ran out of arrows. The Parthian army was now developed along traditional Iranian lines. Infantry was retained for fighting in hill country and for garrisons. But cavalry now became the main arm, divided into two principal types: the horse-archers, and the heavily armed cavalry, the *clibanarii* and the *cataphractii*, who used the huge lance and the bow. The heavy cavalrymen were armour-plated from head to foot, and their horses too wore iron mail. Silver and gold adornments were added. The weight of the armour was limited only by the fact that the horsemen rode without stirrups (and had therefore to be able to grip with the knees), and by the strength of the horse. To supply the tremendous mounts needed for such cavalry, the Parthians bred, from the fine Nesaean chargers that roamed the plains of Media, great war-horses that were the envy of the Chinese and a splendid gift to the Sasanians. This heavy cavalry became in time the armament of Asia. But in the hands of a brilliant commander the horse-archers too could become a fearsome weapon. The heavy cavalry could charge fully armed infantry with effect, but the loss of life among nobles and horses

Fig. 6

was considerable. Mobile horse-archers with powerful long-range bows could inflict equally serious losses without trouble. The feigned retreat and the backward shot over the crupper – the 'Parthian' shot, in fact a traditional Asian manoeuvre – were available in the case of an enemy charge. When Suren added to these advantages an enormous reserve supply of camel-borne arrows, a thing which no commander seems to have done before him, the Parthians gained a force that on level ground could surround and totally defeat an army of heavily armed legionaries more than three times its size with trifling loss. Why, then, was the astounding success of Carrhae never repeated against later Roman invaders? The answer lies in the 'feudal' aspects of the developed Parthian state. The standing army available to the monarch can never have been large or important, at any rate from about 100 BC onwards. The main forces of the Empire consisted of the retainers, the 'dependants and slaves' of the great landowners, who followed their lords to battle; mounted, these provided the Parthian cavalry, and on foot the infantry. Such conditions had obtained in Iran for centuries. When war was declared, the king of kings summoned his sub-kings and governors, who joined him with their followers. It was difficult to keep such an army together for a campaign that lasted longer than a season, and sieges were rarely successful: Seleucia held out for seven years against Artabanus III and Vardanes, and then surrendered voluntarily. The troops felt greater loyalty to their individual noble commanders than to the king. The signal for battle was given on the kettle-drums, and then normally they fought in the traditional manner. Special training, if they received any, was in the hands of the landowners. Suren built up some ten thousand of his retainers into a formidable private army, and defeated Crassus with few horsemen who were not his own. But Suren's ability and far-sightedness were exceptional, even frightening. With an army command as a whole so variable in quality and loyalty, with a weak central control over the Empire's military resources, such triumphs were likely to be rare. Moreover, success such as Suren's was to be feared; the year after Carrhae, he was executed by order of Orodes. His tactical ideas were thenceforth largely neglected, and mercenaries again began to form a significant part of the Parthian forces.

The nomad background of the Parthians, so evident in their military tactics, influenced other aspects of official life. Capitals and residences, between which the court seems constantly to have been moving, proliferated. The first capital of the Parthians was perhaps Nisa, where Isidorus of Charax notes the existence of royal tombs. The town of Dara, near Abivard, was founded according to Justin as a capital by the second Arsaces, but the site was found to be unsuitable and for the next capital the town of Hecatompylus was chosen. This change occurred before the campaign of Antiochus III at the end of the third century BC, and it is the as yet undiscovered Hecatompylus which many classical writers regard as the Parthians' royal city. The city of Asaak was also prominent in the early history of Parthia: there, says Isidorus, 'Arsaces' was proclaimed king and an eternal fire burned. Then under Mithradates a garrison was installed in Babylonia at the village of Ctesiphon, to watch the Greek city of Seleucia on the opposite bank of the Tigris. Pacorus, the son of Orodes II, is said by Ammianus Marcellinus to have made Ctesiphon 'the crowning ornament of Persia' – that is, to have turned it into the great winter capital of the Parthians. Finally, Vologasias was founded near Seleucia to divert trade from the Greek city, but its period as a capital seems scarcely to have outlasted its founder, Vologases I. The court could now pass the seasons in Ctesiphon, Ecbatana, Rhagae and Hecatompylus, just as the Achaemenid kings had moved between Susa, Persepolis and Ecbatana.

The king must have been assisted by secretaries, officials and clerks, but the central administration failed to impose any simple uniformity in administration throughout the Empire. Where the royal archives were kept is unknown, although local record offices certainly existed. Chinese visitors noticed merely that documents were written sideways (rather than vertically) and on parchment. Language presented a problem. The official languages of the Achaemenid Persians had been three: Old Persian, Elamite and Akkadian, with Aramaic as a widely used *lingua franca*. Persian is an Indo-European language, of the Indo-Iranian or *satem* sub-family. The language spoken by the Parni was a northern dialect of Middle Persian with archaic features, known sometimes as Arsacid Pahlavi and described by Justin as 'a mixture of Scythian and Median'. Yet the Arsacids adopted Greek, the language of Seleucid bureaucracy, as their first official language. Indeed, many of them are known to have been able to speak it. This was the language of their coinage, of the inscriptions of Mithradates II and Gotarzes II, and of their correspondence with such cities as Susa. Squared letter forms came into use for Greek inscriptions long before Roman engravers adopted them. Greek was also widely used for semi-official and private documents of every kind. Throughout western Parthia, the Semitic language Aramaic was widespread. Cursive Aramaic scripts were in common use, and in some centres, such as Palmyra, the script became clear and elegant. Bilingual inscriptions in Aramaic and Greek are commonly found, and when the Romans took Aramaic-speaking cities of the Parthian fringe, trilingual inscriptions were sometimes engraved. The Parthian language itself occurs more rarely than Greek or Aramaic. The Aramaic script is used, a practice introduced for Old Persian by Darius, but now for the most part the language is written heterographically with Aramaic words as well. Such heterographic systems were not unusual in the ancient Near East. The Aramaic script, however, has the same disability as many Asian scripts, ancient and modern, that basically consonants together with only two

Fig. 10

Fig. 11

Fig. 10

68

A	B	C	D	E
				ʾ
				b
				g
				d
				h
				w
				z
				ḥ
				ṭ
				y
				k
				l
				m
				n (final)
				s
				ʿ
				p
				ṣ
				q
				r
				š (sh)
				t

Fig. 10   Aramaic alphabets
(A) Elephantine manuscripts, fifth century BC; (B) Palmyra, early first century AD;
(C) Palmyra, early third century AD; (D) Palmyra, cursive; (E) Transcription

69

Plate 5

Fig. 12

long vowels are represented. Vocalisation therefore presents a problem, particularly where non-Semitic tongues are concerned. The Aramaic words in the Parthian documents would have been 'read' as Parthian words. Thus in the Avroman parchment, the script and the majority of the words are Aramaic, but the remaining words and a termination are Parthian, and the document must have been read as Parthian. Furthermore, over two thousand potsherds from Nisa, mostly of the first century BC, bear inscriptions wholly in Aramaic script and vocabulary, but were almost undoubtedly 'read' as Parthian. Paradoxically, Parthian does not appear publicly as an official language until a late stage in Parthian history, and was not in common official use until the Sasanian era. It is used tentatively on certain coins from the first century AD onwards; then, in AD 215, Artabanus V honours Khwasak, satrap of Susa, in a Parthian

Fig. 11   Trilingual inscription from Palmyra in Latin, Greek and Aramaic, commemorating the building of a tomb by Hairan the son of Bonne, and dated April, AD 52. Ht 33½ in. (85 cm.). (From Syria, *1950, p. 137 f., fig. 1).*

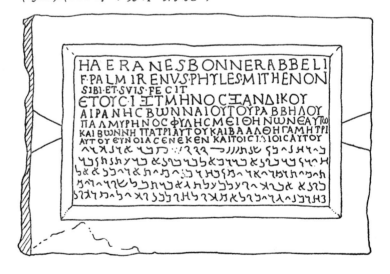

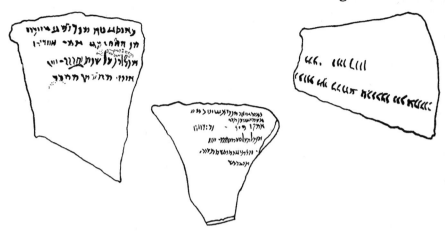

Fig. 12   Three ostraca *from Nisa with texts in Aramaic script, used perhaps as labels for wine jars and dated in the earlier first century* BC. *About 1 :2 (After* Vestnik Drevnei Istorii, *1954, 2, figs. 1–3)*

inscription. Minority languages of the Empire included the living and defunct tongues of Babylonia still written in cuneiform script until, at least, 6 BC, and of course Hebrew. In the Syrian and Mesopotamian deserts, Arabic was spoken. For every significant language, the king must have maintained special secretaries; a letter from Artabanus III to Susa, dated AD 21, reveals that the Greek secretaries knew their Hellenistic protocol.

Parthian methods of dating were unnecessarily complicated. The normal Seleucid era, for which the years were counted from autumn (1 Dios or Hyperberetaios) 312 BC, was widely used, and adopted for the official coinage. A variant on this was employed in Babylonia, where the New Year festival was held in spring and the Seleucid era was reckoned from the spring (1 Nisan) 311 BC. Then a royal Arsacid era, used by the kings, was introduced, and seems usually to have been counted, like the variant Seleucid, from the spring. This era began with 247 BC. It was used at Nisa, and also in western

Parthia, where many documents bear a double date, as communities refused to abandon the Seleucid era. Thus a parchment contract from Dura begins: 'In the reign of Arsaces, King of kings, ... year 368 according to the reckoning of the King of kings, but according to the former [Seleucid] reckoning, 432, on the twenty-sixth day of the month Daisios...' (AD 121). The earliest known use of the Arsacid era appears on a double-dated document of 141 BC from Babylon. The variety of lunar months used with these eras – Macedonian Greek, Babylonian, Aramaic, Iranian and Zoroastrian – which differed with language and area, complicated matters further. To establish the year of Parthian documents dated by unspecified eras can be troublesome.

A similar complexity was probably also present in the system of taxation, about which very little is known. Presumably, at first the Seleucid system was adopted, itself a medley of older and newer practices. Land taxes were seemingly collected by provincial governors and sent to the central treasury, whereas other types of tax – customs duties, taxes on slaves, salt and so on – were the responsibility of special royal tax officials. Cities apparently collected their own taxes and sent them in separately. Levies and war booty added to the royal revenues. Manesus, the governor, or *strategos*, of Mesopotamia and Parapotamia in AD 121, collected taxes among his many other duties. Documents from Seleucia mention a variety of taxes, on salt, on the sale of slaves, on transport by river and so on. Later evidence, of which much is given in the Talmud, may reflect the conditions towards the end of Parthian rule. There seems to have been a land tax, and a poll tax that was not paid by the upper ranks of society. Towns perhaps continued to be treated separately. Once a man was registered at a town or village, he paid his taxes there regularly. When these sources of revenue proved insufficient for the expenses of the royal treasury, the special levy always lay to hand.

Fig. 13   Sketch of parchment II from Avroman partly unrolled, showing the method of sealing the interior section. (From Journal of Hellenic Studies, *1915, fig. 1)*

Parthian law is again largely a mystery. Presumably the monarch alone was the fount of legislation. It is quite clear, however, from the few relevant documents that survive, that older Oriental and Hellenistic practices continued almost unaltered for centuries under Parthian rule, and no important innovations are discernible in theory or practice. In western Parthia, Babylonian practice still survived. Babylonian law, for instance, whereby loans could be arranged on the security of almost anything, from pottery to land, house, family or the debtor's person, underlies the parchment contract of AD 121 from Dura. Here a certain Barlaas is loaned a large sum of money for one year on the security of his property: instead of paying interest, he undertakes to work for the lender, one Phraates. The actual language and formulae of the document are, however, Hellenistic Greek, with Graeco-Egyptian parallels. The contract is carefully dated, and names of witnesses appended. Older too is the comparatively common method of drawing up 'duplicate' texts of legal documents, with 'close' and 'patent' versions. The 'close' version is rolled up and sealed, and is only to be opened and consulted if any query arises over the open and theoretically identical 'patent' version. Typical of this are parchments I and II in Greek from Avroman in Kurdistan. The sale of a vine-

Fig. 13

yard in the village Copanis forms the subject. The documents are compiled in a thoroughly slapdash manner, and the close and patent versions differ frequently over minor points – even the price. Nevertheless, Hellenistic practice forms the basis of these documents. A third parchment in Parthian (as is a short endorsement of parchment I) is concerned with the same vine⁄ yard, but lacks the detailed arrangements of the first two. The three documents are dated in the years 225, 291, and 300 – but by which era(s) are they reckoned? Copies of deeds like these were generally kept in city archives. The rescript of Artabanus III to the city of Susa, a stone inscription written in Greek and double⁄dated AD 21, records the settlement of a contested mun⁄ icipal election by the king. Again, language and formulae are Hellenistic Greek. A royal court, and royal judges with re⁄ sounding titles, are mentioned in the parchments of Dura, and fines were payable both to injured parties and to the 'palace'. Punishments were sometimes severe. In a mud wall of Seleucia a man had been buried alive. In struggling vainly to break free, he broke his spine. This smacks of rough justice.

The Parthian coinage was also derived from Hellenistic Greek prototypes. Until the period of Mithradates I, the Par⁄ thians minted no coins of their own, and must have used Seleucid issues. For their coins, like the Seleucids, they adopt⁄ ed the Attic Greek standard of weight and metal. Silver and bronze coins only were minted. Seleucid gold continued to circulate for a while after the Parthian conquest, but was not replaced. The extent to which older issues continued to cir⁄ culate is well illustrated by a hoard of silver coins buried in Mesene soon after 45/4 BC. A wide selection is represented, running back to Athenian coins of the fifth century BC! Par⁄ thian silver coins were issued in two primary denominations: the drachm, and the rarer quadruple coin, the tetradrachm. Bronze issues included a wide range of sizes and weights. The currency was issued by the Parthian king from various mints

Plate 5

Plate 6

within the Empire, and by his sub-kings from their capitals. Many mints placed a special monogram on their coins. Certain communities, notably Seleucia, also issued their own municipal coinage. Seleucid types formed the basic repertoire of coin motifs, but significant alterations included the replacement of Apollo on the reverse by an enigmatic seated figure with a bow. The king's head, in varying headgear, always appears on the obverse, usually in profile but occasionally frontal. Curiously, Chinese travellers reported that the face of the king's consort always appeared on the reverse: this happened only during the reigns of Phraataces and Gotarzes II. Greek was the official language for the legends, and dates, where they appear, are given according to the normal Seleucid calendar. The king himself exercised a certain control over his coinage, as the insertion of the word Philhellene by Mithradates I and its deletion by Artabanus III for political reasons indicates. Aramaic lettering begins to supplement the increasingly barbarised Greek legends of the reverse from the reign of Vologases I onwards. Most coins of the sub-kings closely imitate those of their overlord. But in some areas, such as Persis and Elymais, a certain independence was shown in the choice of motifs and language. When the quality of the silver currency began to deteriorate seriously in the early second century AD – to be frank, the coins became simply silver-washed bronze – purer Roman coins were sometimes used for a transaction. 'Good Tyrian silver' (that is, Roman coinage), for instance, was stipulated for the loan to Barlaas at Dura. Events of importance sometimes received commemoration by words and scenes, but the Parthians were not so sophisticated in their use of coins for the spreading of political propaganda as were the Romans.

Plate 6gg

There were many weaknesses in the Parthian system of government. Had the later Parthian rulers called in constitutional advisers from the Roman Empire, the Romans could have pointed out some of these. The small size of the army that was directly under royal control, and the hereditary nature and the power of the positions of sub-kings and satraps, contributed greatly towards internal instability. The people were bound together by no ties of elaborately graded citizenship. The organisation of the royal succession lacked the extreme care taken by the Romans. Yet what was right for Rome would not necessarily have worked well among her neighbours. The Parthians, to misquote Cicero's remark concerning Carthage, 'would not have held an Empire for five hundred years had it not been governed with wisdom and statecraft'.

CHAPTER V

Economics and Society

AGRICULTURE AND TRADE together formed the basis of Parthian economics; industry played only a minor role. The majority of the inhabitants of the Empire gained their live-lihood by working on the land, as independent farmers or herdsmen, as 'serfs' of the great landowners, or probably in some cases as slaves. Sheep, goats, cattle, pigs, horses, asses and Arabian camels were raised, and cereal crops, rice, fruit and vegetables grown. Most of the cultivable areas of the Empire required irrigation to supplement the insufficient supplies of water from river and rainfall. Irrigation therefore assumed an immense importance in the agriculture of western Asia. In Iran proper, water was often conducted through underground chan-nels. Such *qanats* Artabanus I tried to destroy as he retreated to-wards Parthia before Antiochus III. Zamaspes, satrap of Susa in AD 1/2, was honoured with a statue and an inscription in verse for bringing the water of the river Gondeisos to the lands of Susa. Minute details of the arrangements over the water rights of the vineyard at Copanis are set down in the Avroman parchments. A close study of the Diyala region of Iraq has shown what was achieved by the intelligent use of water re-sources in antiquity. The Seleucid and Parthian periods saw immense improvements in the region. Animal traction was now almost certainly ued to raise water for irrigation, and whole networks of canals carried the water further and further away from the main rivers. Dredging and upkeep are naturally im-plied by such extensive works. Gardens full of date palms must already have lined the river banks of Babylonia.

Plate 7

As the over-all picture of trade movement between the Medi-terranean and the Near and Far East after the Seleucid collapse became clear, the Parthians emerged primarily as middlemen,

Fig. 14

rather than as producers. In the early period, the Parthians doubtless traded with Seleucid businessmen. Commercial contacts with China were firmly established before the end of the second century BC. Ch'ang Ch'ien and others reported the Parthians' eagerness to trade. Their wagons, caravans and ships travelled to neighbouring lands, and they sent exotic presents, ostrich eggs and conjurers, to excite the interest of the Chinese emperor. The Silk Route between China and the Mediterranean came into use. Friendly embassies and presents continue to be mentioned in Chinese sources in the first and second centuries AD. The Chinese were familiar with Parthian coins, and a Parthian coin legend was copied as the decoration for a Chinese bronze before AD 150. With India, Parthia's commercial contacts are less well documented. Indian coins, however, adopted the square form of the Greek letter *omicron* at the same time in the first century BC as did the Parthian. Eventually Parthia was linked by land to the great route from Bactra to Barygaza, and by means of the sea route from Spasinu Charax to the Indus mouth, a journey of at least forty days. To the north of Iran, Parthian coins have been found over a wide area, and art objects in south Russia, especially at Olbia, where an important series of carved ivories was discovered. On the west, after 70–60 BC, lay the Roman Empire. Besides the normal routes from Babylonia to northern Syria, a short cut for caravans across the Syrian desert became popular from this time by way of the Roman oasis town of Palmyra. Here vast numbers of inscriptions illuminate trade routes of the area. Many western

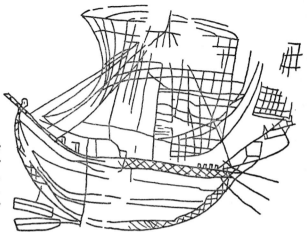

Fig. 14 Graffiti from private houses of Dura Europos illustrating trade by caravan and ship. Second or early third century AD. (After M. Rostovtzeff, Caravan Cities, figs. 5–6)

Parthian cities were regularly visited by Palmyrenes, from perhaps Hatra in Mesopotamia to Babylon, Seleucia, Vologasias and Spasinu Charax in Babylonia and Mesene. Further afield, Susa, and even north-west India (called 'Scythia', on account of the Saca or 'Scythian' tribesmen now installed there) are mentioned.

Within Parthia, further routes are known. The most important linked the two ends of the Silk Route. Stopping-places or caravanserais along this route are indicated in Isidorus' *Parthian Stations*, written *c*. 1 BC or *c*. AD 70. Isidorus guides us from Antioch on the Orontes across the Euphrates and Parthian frontier at Zeugma, and then south-east to Seleucia (which took at least fifteen days). Next we turn north-east to Ecbatana, Rhagae, Nisa and Merv. Thence Isidorus leads us through erstwhile Parthian territory via southern Afghanistan to the border of India. But the Chinese branch of this route, ignored by Isidorus, forked off beyond Merv at Bactra (Balkh), the 'Mother of Cities', whence it passed to the Stone Tower (Tashkurgan), Turfan, through Chinese Turkestan and so to China itself. Numerous lesser roads and alternative routes branched out

Fig. 15

from the main artery in the eastern sector beyond Parthia and particularly also in the western Parthian region, so that our map gives only the general direction of routes taken. An important route of western Parthia naturally linked Spasinu Charax with Seleucia. A road ran north from here to Hatra, where Maishan (Mesene) is mentioned. The coins found at Susa were minted mainly at Susa itself, at Seleucia or at Spasinu Charax, and indicate a busy traffic along this route. Lastly, Strabo repeatedly speaks of another route, from Persepolis to Carmania, and in-deed a Parthian village set into granite rocks was discovered near Kerman. Logically, this route should continue via Seistan to India, but no evidence as yet confirms this.

A passage in the official Chinese records has often been quot-ed to show that the great overland Silk Route was closed or menaced for long periods by a hostile Parthian government. This is nonsense. The passage in the *Han-shu* runs: '[The Ro-man emperors] always desired to send embassies to China, but the An-hsi [Parthians] wished to carry on trade with them in Chinese silks, and it is for this reason that they were cut off from communication. This lasted till [AD 166], when the king of Ta-ts'in [Roman Empire], An-tun [Marcus Aurelius Antoni-nus] sent an embassy... From that time dates the direct inter-course with this country.' Now all that the Chinese actually say is that the Parthians did not allow them to *communicate* directly with the Romans. The Parthians were not so blind to their own self-interests as to destroy the east-west trade that brought them such revenues. They merely held their two great-est customers firmly apart, to avoid any embarrassing compari-son of prices. Both Chinese and Palmyrene records show a constant and peaceful traffic into Parthian territory that made nonsense of political policies and boundaries. Admittedly, in-ternal disturbances and Roman attacks on the western frontiers must have rendered the Route unsafe or impassable from time to time, but never for long: economic interests usually outweigh political. If final proof that the Silk Route remained open were needed, it is provided by the richness of the archaeological dis‑ coveries made on the sites of commercial cities from end to end of the Parthian Empire. At Palmyra and at Hatra, spectacular buildings still stand; at these and at other sites, from Merv and Nisa to Susa, Seleucia, Assur and elsewhere, architectural and artistic discoveries have been made of sufficient importance to demand separate chapters in this book. Nor would the Parthian kings have had reliefs carved at Behistun had no one been pass‑ ing by to see them. Older towns continued to prosper, new ones arose from villages or even, like Hatra and Vologasias, from nothing. Numerous sculptures from the western Parthian area also testify to the wealth of these city merchants and princes, whose well‑fed forms and ample abdomens have been preserv‑ ed for all time in statuary.

Plates 45, 54

The actual working methods of the caravan traders are illu‑ minated by the inscriptions of Palmyra. A typical example, once placed beneath an honorary statue, runs: 'This is the statue of Taimarsu the son of Taima... the caravan chief. It was raised to him by the caravan men who came up with him from Spasinu Charax, because he lent them 300 gold *denarii* of the old weight, and was agreeable to them. To honour him and his sons... in the month Nisan, 504' (April, AD 193). Taimarsu, and many others like him, promoted trade by lending money and by ensuring the protection of caravans and merchants in many ways, sometimes (as here) by leading the caravans per‑ sonally. The Durene official who was *Arabarch* would also have been responsible for policing the desert and protecting traders. The Chinese noted that the merchants of Roman Syria were honest, and gained a tenfold profit from their trade with Parthia and India.

Some idea of the commodities involved in this trade can be drawn from contemporary documents and archaeological dis‑ coveries. The long inscription known as the Tariff of Palmyra

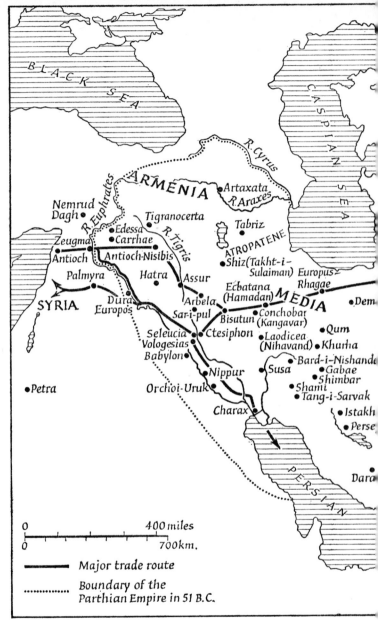

Fig. 15   *Towns, sites and trade routes of the Parthian Empire*

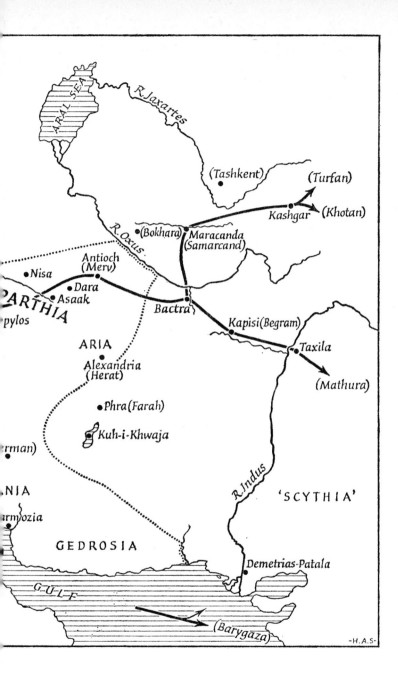

ARAL SEA

R. Jaxartes

(Tashkent)

(Turfan)

(Khotan)

Kashgar

R. Oxus

(Bokhara)

Maracanda
(Samarcand)

Antioch
(Merv)

Nisa

Dara
Asaak

PARTHIA

pylos

Bactra

Kapisi (Begram)

Taxila

(Mathura)

ARIA

Alexandria
(Herat)

Phra (Farah)

Kuh-i-Khwaja

R. Indus

'SCYTHIA'

rman)

NIA

rmozia

GEDROSIA

Demetrias-Patala

G·U·L·F

(Barygaza)

-H.A.S-

83

Fig. 14

and dated AD 137 gives the local municipal taxes on imported goods. A camel-load is the basic unit of measurement; a wagon-load is reckoned the equivalent of four laden camels, and a donkey-load as half a camel-load. Slaves, dried fruits, purple dye, perfumes (carefully distinguished), olive oil, fat, animals and skins, salt, foodstuffs, pine-cones and bronze statues all appear as articles of trade. Chinese records add exotic animals, gold, silver, precious stones, rugs, 'all kinds of fragrant substances', fine cloth and of course Chinese silks. From China the Parthians also imported Seric iron, the apricot and the peach, and in return sent goods which included the vine, pomegranates, ostriches and other unusual items. A fragment of Isidorus' lost *Description of Parthia* reports on the industry concerned with gathering another prized commodity, the pearls of the Persian Gulf. The *Periplus of the Erythraean Sea*, a handbook compiled around AD 60 for merchant seamen sailing between Egypt and India, mentions cargoes of rare woods, cloth, dye and spices. In proof of these reports, the tombs and city of Palmyra, Dura and elsewhere have yielded fragments of woven silk and silk yarn from China, Indian cloth, glassware and stones both precious and of glass paste. The Hellenistic figurines of Nisa, moreover, like the Roman metalwork, glassware, and plaster casts from Begram in Afghanistan, may well have travelled great distances by the ever-moving caravans.

This is a luxury trade. Some light is thrown by it upon Parthian economics, wherein certain parallels with the economic system of the Roman west emerge. Wealth was concentrated at the top of society. The members of the upper classes were the chief consumers, and they made comparatively few demands. Consequently the society as a whole was not stimulated into large-scale manufacture; there was no incentive to create machinery. Slaves were there to perform simple and repetitive tasks, and therefore technical skill remained minimal. The rare evidence of such skill includes a curious ovoid pottery jar found in

Babylonia. It contained copper, iron and bitumen, and was probably once used as a galvanic cell for electroplating silver on to copper. Large workshops must of course have existed for the production of such day-to-day essentials as pottery, but the processes involved were still extremely simple. Transport was costly and slow, and involved dangers from war, brigands and wild animals. Thus although humble items such as pottery jars of oil and wine were sometimes carried considerable distances – fragments of jars with stamps from the Greek islands Rhodes and Thasos were found at Nimrud, Susa and Seleucia – only goods likely to bring in a rich return formed the real stuff of trade. Moreover, the Parthian Empire as a whole was economically unbalanced in favour of the western portion. This imbalance had political repercussions: Babylonia was a favourite springboard for usurpers. But the flourishing of art and architecture attest very wide prosperity from about 50 BC, when the Romans had settled Syria, to AD 150. The abandonment of the use of tetradrachms, however, and the serious depreciation of the silver coinage from the first century AD onwards, warn us that economic conditions were worsening. By AD 200, damage wrought by Romans, the decline of many cities, including Babylon, Seleucia, Assur and Susa, and the utter debasement of the coinage indicate widespread decay. But the ships and caravans continued to ply, if some routes altered course; no significant change in price-level is discernible between 113 BC and AD 164 at Dura, and Hatra, Palmyra and other cities remained prosperous.

At the head of Parthian society stood the king. Normally, he was inaccessible. His throne was golden; he slept on a golden couch. Those granted an audience had to bring a gift. On the coins we see the royal headdress change from the pointed Saca cap to a simple diadem, and then into a high bejewelled tiara. Vassals imitated these headdresses, but it is clear from the reliefs of Nemrud Dagh in Commagene (*c.* 69–34 BC) that the shapes

Plates 6, 30, 31, 50–52

and ornament were all meaningful and carefully distinguished. A torque encircled the king's neck, and his costume was elaborately adorned. His subjects, according to Justin and Plutarch, were divided into a minority of freemen and a large number of dependants or slaves; these writers were, however, describing the army. The basis of Iranian society at large was the extended family or clan and tribe. The freemen, or *azatan*, comprised the sub-kings, nobles, royal officials and their families. The dependants and slaves are the followers of the nobles, peasants who are bound to the land they farm, or 'serfs'. There is little evidence of true slavery in Parthia (if we except the predominantly Greek border town of Dura), although it must have existed; perhaps the later distinction between slaves captured in war and persons sold for debt already applied. But as a whole, slavery was less significant in Parthia than 'serfdom'. These 'feudal' conditions applied above all to the Iranian sector of society, in its various groupings. The now dominant Arsacids were sprung from the northern group of Iranians. In Persis another group was established, which spoke a south-western dialect of middle

Plate 6l, ll Persian derived from the Old Persian of the Achaemenid era. Here a number of old Persian traditions were maintained, as the coinage of the princes shows. As vassals of the Seleucids, their coins continue to resemble Achaemenid issues, and a fire

Plate 6n, nn temple and the winged symbol of the ancient god Ahura Mazda appear. Under Parthian domination, the Parthian coinage is imitated, but Greek is never used. Aramaic, and later heterographic Middle Persian, are employed for the legends. The rulers call themselves 'king', and their names, Darius and Artaxerxes among them, recall an earlier imperial grandeur.

Side by side with the Iranians lived other peoples and communities. Western Parthia was dominated by Aramaeans, people of Semitic speech who inhabited the towns and plains, and who lived as far east as Elymais. In the towns of Babylonia lived the Babylonians, Semites also. Out in the desert under the watchful eyes of the Parthian authorities wandered the Arabs. They were gradually infiltrating into the settled communities of western Asia, and have since of course become dominant over a wide part of the Near East. Half the personal names at Palmyra, for instance, are already Arabic, whereas the first language of the city was still Aramaic, and the rulers of Hatra bear the title 'king of the Arabs' in the local Aramaic inscriptions. The Jews formed a further Semitic element. They were recognised as a community by the Parthians and given a certain local autonomy. They were numerous in western Parthia, as emerges from the Talmud, particularly in northern Babylonia, and others were scattered across Iran. The head of their community was responsible for collecting taxes, appointing their judges and other tasks. Jews were permitted to inflict the death penalty on members of their own community. They were in close contact with their kinsmen in Palestine.

Greeks lived in the towns, particularly those founded by Alexander and the Seleucids, from end to end of the Empire. In some communities they, and their civilisation and language, remained dominant, at any rate until the first century AD. They formed so powerful an element in the Empire that successive rulers from the time of Mithradates II deemed it wise to include in their titles the epithet Philhellene. Artabanus III, in disapproval of the Greek communities, struck this word out of his coin-titles, although his successors soon reinstated it.

Plate 6ii

The Parthians were also great town-builders, according to Ammianus Marcellinus, and the names of Ctesiphon, Vologasias, Hatra and the rebuilt Nisa and Merv spring to mind. Even the greatest of Parthian cities would, however, look small today. The probable population of Seleucia, given as 600,000 by Pliny, is reduced to a mere 80,000 by a recent estimate based upon excavation. In all these communities, whether ancient, or founded by Greeks or Iranians, the actual populations were extremely mixed, in both race and political outlook. The names of the kings of Mesene reflect a wide variety of Greek and Oriental ethnic groups, of which no doubt their subjects were composed. Mercantile communities such as Palmyra maintained depots and establishments of their fellow Palmyrenes in the main commercial cities of western Parthia – in Babylon, all Seleucia, Spasinu Charax, Vologasias and elsewhere. At Dura Europos a medley of Greek, Semitic and Iranian names is recorded, and this mixture was surely characteristic of many city populations of this cosmopolitan Empire. Admittedly, many of these communities long retained a particular identity – Greek, Babylonian, Assyrian and so on; at Nisa, Iranian names in plenty occur on the inscribed *ostraca*. But only in villages and tribes were ethnic identities fully preserved.

Of Parthian society and daily life, the ancient writers and archaeological discoveries give us isolated snapshots, as it were. Parthia was a man's world, as are most Asian communities. Justin delightedly lists the Parthians' supposed bad characteristics. They were arrogant, treacherous and violent, and always causing disturbances. Yet, we learn, they were silent by nature, and quicker to act than to talk. Women were shut away in their own quarters, and the royal concubines were surrounded by guards and eunuchs. No woman was allowed to dine with her husband, nor even to be publicly seen, declares Justin.

Plate 35 Imagination has doubtless coloured Justin's account, but there
Plate 44 are signs of female restriction. From the Dura legal documents it emerges that women were normally illiterate. Semitic women already wore the veil, although it is represented as pulled across the face only on religious occasions. Affection for children is reflected in the memorials inspired by premature death.

Most houses, as we shall see, were of mud brick and built
Fig. 16 around a courtyard, as they often are today. At night, numerous little oil lamps provided light. The pots and jars of Parthia
Plate 9 at first imitated oriental and Seleucid wares. Gradually, how-
Fig. 17 ever, the refinement of the Greek shapes melted away and pot-

Fig. 16 *Interior court of house Y at Assur, showing the vaulting and the flat roof reached by a staircase. Early third century* AD. *(After W. Andrae,* Die Partherstadt Assur, *fig. 2)*

tery grew coarser. Decoration in the form of grooves, patterns and ornamental heads was applied. Glazes, usually blue or green but sometimes yellow or brown, were now often added. The toy pottery and the money-boxes with coin slots found at Seleucia have a modern look. Sometimes vessels of real quality were made. A good marble vase was found at Susa, and some fine rhytons or drinking horns of a shape derived from those of Achaemenid times at Nisa and Demavend. The Parthians were great drinkers, but, according to Justin, sparing in their consumption of food. At Nisa, large numbers of potsherds, mostly of the first century BC, were discovered in and around wine stores. These *ostraca* were perhaps once placed as labels on wine jars. Not only do they record the quantity and year of the vintage, but sometimes even the vineyard. Vinegar and raisins are also mentioned on them. A speciality wherever dates grew was palm wine. The Parthians ate meat obtained through hunting, bread both leavened and unleavened, fresh and dried fruit, and vegetables; those who could get it had fish. They knew the properties of all manner of herbs and spices, but nothing is known of their cuisine.

Plates 8, 10
Fig. 42

Fig. 12

The aristocratic and mercantile classes of society enjoyed high standards of living derived from commerce and from exploitation of the peasantry. Flamboyant statues proclaim their superiority. Heroic nudity could be left for the portrayal of the leaders of Greek and Roman society. Parthian statuary is above all a vehicle for the display of wealth and luxurious personal adornment. Like the Parthian monarch himself, the kings of Hatra wear a lofty, pearl-encrusted headdress. Their tunics and trous-

Plates 50, 52, 65

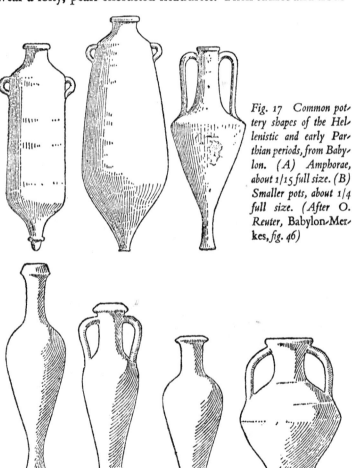

Fig. 17 *Common pottery shapes of the Hellenistic and early Parthian periods, from Babylon. (A) Amphorae, about 1/15 full size. (B) Smaller pots, about 1/4 full size. (After O. Reuter, Babylon-Merkes, fig. 46)*

Fig. 18   Inlaid gold buckle or harness decoration with the scene of an eagle tearing a young animal. Length 3½in. (9 cm.). British Museum

ers too are covered with jewels. Great decorated belts encircle their waists, and sometimes an elaborate coat is worn over the whole ensemble. At Palmyra, embroidery runs riot over the tunics of men and women alike. Trousers were a nomad garment, suitable for riding and for the lower temperatures of much nomad territory. When worn in hotter areas, the costume of tunic and trousers could be made of finer material. Leggings of leather or cloth were added for riding, and were held up by a complicated system of straps, and a dagger worn at the side completed the Parthian costume. In the western Parthian regions, many men wore Greek dress, the tunic *(chiton)* and cloak *(himation)*, looser garments more suitable for the hotter weather. None of these costumes was suitable for farmers or workmen. Such persons are not normally shown in Parthian art, but at Palmyra they wore a short tunic, to which might be added a peculiar garment which was wrapped around the legs somewhat in the manner of a sarong. From the time of Mithradates I, Parthian men were often bearded. The hair was usually worn long and is shown elaborately dressed in wavy locks or tiered curls. Women were well-wrapped, as is customary in western Asia. They wore an ankle-length tunic, a cloak which could be thrown over the head, and often a veil as well that normally hung at the back of the head. Much favoured was a somewhat

Fig. 18
Plate 4

Plate 30

Plate 34

Plates 42, 43, 45
46
complex headdress consisting of a metal diadem and a high
turban over which the cloak or veil was placed. Their hair was
normally dressed in the Greek manner with a central parting.

Plate 11
Jewellery added to the effect. Many elaborate pieces continued
to be made in the Hellenistic Greek style. But silver bracelets
with granulations, other items with silver wire-work and beaded
decoration (as found at Dura), and a new emphasis on
colour constituted Parthian innovations. In Syria, the glass fac-
Plates 42, 45
tories turned out ornaments of glass paste which were incorporated into flexible chains for necklaces and bracelets. Amulets
also abounded. The well-dressed Parthian women vied in
quantity of jewellery with the most exotic of Edwardian beau-
ties. Men, too, loaded their fingers with rings and their garments
and soft shoes with stones and pearls. The wearing of earrings
by men, however, tended to be a rustic, not a metropolitan,
Fig. 19
Plate 42
custom. The final touches to the appearance were put in with
cosmetics. Traces of colouring on Palmyrene funerary reliefs indicate that the 'Beauty of Palmyra', for instance, wore red lip-
stick, drew black lines around her eyes, and rouged her cheeks.
Men, too, used cosmetics: Suren, the conqueror of Crassus,
scandalised the Romans with his painted face and effeminately
dressed hair. The kings and Magi, according to Pliny, used a
decoction of the plant *helianthes* in lion's fat, with saffron and
palm wine added, as an ointment to improve their appearance –
one hopes they found it efficacious. A still more elaborate ointment, with twenty-seven ingredients, was used at the coronation. Perfume completed the toilet: perfume jars were discovered at Seleucia.

In their palaces and large merchants' houses, the Parthian
Plates 12–14
rich used gold and silverware of the finest quality. Bowls are
decorated with leaf motifs, laurel, acanthus and vine, or with
rosettes and figures. Forms derived from both the Achaemenid
and Seleucid eras can be distinguished. The decoration of a
Plate 15
box found at Shami consisted of figures in mother-of-pearl in-

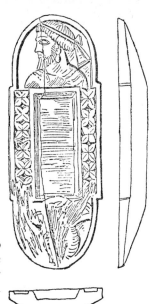

Fig. 19   Slate palette for cosmetics, decorated with the heads of a ruler and queen in imitation of coin portraits. Probably first century BC *or* AD. *Slightly less than actual size. (After E. Herzfeld,* Iran in the Ancient East, *fig. 396)*

lay. Musical instruments were played, including the lyre, the single pipe, the double-pipe and the drum. On the walls of palaces hung figured tapestries, if we are to believe Philostratus, and both walls and floors were doubtless covered with the finest carpets. The discoveries of a resplendent carpet of the fourth century BC with Achaemenian motifs, found frozen in the fifth chieftain's tomb at Pazyryk in south Russia, and of a pile rug fragment at Dura, together with the survival of carpet-making until our own day, must mean that the Parthians also practised this noble art.

The pursuits of the Parthian monarch and nobility were typical of many Indo-European aristocracies. As befitted their nomad background, much of their life was spent on horseback. 'On horses they go to war, to banquets, to public and private tasks,' writes Justin, 'and on them they travel, stay still, do business and chat.' Only 'slaves' go on foot. Their chief love was

Plates 4, 69

the hunt. So enthusiastic were they for this pursuit, that king Vardanes even tactlessly offered the emaciated philosopher Apollonius of Tyana a day's hunting near Babylon. Wild animals were often kept penned up in a park or 'paradise'. No monarch was acceptable who did not love horses and the hunt; and Vonones, educated at Rome, was soon rejected for this reason. Artabanus III, when temporarily forced to flee to the regions east of the Caspian, was quite able to support himself by the bow. The Parthian aristocrats probably enjoyed fighting also, for when no outside enemy threatened, internal hostilities frequently broke out. The nobles' panoplies were always elaborate, and it is fascinating to watch the growth of heraldry in the later Parthian period. The various insignia of the aristocrats are plainly represented on the great rock relief of Firuzabad, Plate 75 carved to commemorate the triumph of the Sasanian Ardashir over the last Parthian monarch. The casualties in these internal struggles were probably not normally very great. By the second century AD, the aristocrats were perhaps playing polo in addition to their other pursuits. Feasting was a further pastime of high popularity. At the banquets bards would have sung heroic lays. Whole cycles of these epics existed, like those which underlay the Homeric poems of Greece. These Iranian lays similarly gave rise to a national epic, Firdosi's *Shahnameh,* or Book of Kings. Of a written Parthian literature there is no contemporary evidence, although it is very likely that it existed, and Parthian words entered neighbouring languages. Some of the monarchs favoured Greek culture and had Greek plays performed at court. A Greek theatre was discovered at Nisa, and a performance of Euripides' *Bacchae* was allegedly arranged by king Artavasdes of Armenia for Orodes II.

But an interest in any culture but their own was exceptional among the Parthians, and their own was of a type that left few monuments behind it. What of the fate of these other cultures in the Parthian era? The decline and fall of the cultures of Babylonia, Assyria and Greece in the Parthian period form an absorbing study, for sufficient evidence survives for us to plot the outlines of decline. The cultural influence of Babylonia was widespread and deep in western Parthia. There the Babylonians, city-loving Semites, preserved their ancient ways and religion right into our era. The cuneiform script continued to develop and lasted until 6 BC at least, when clay tablets were finally ousted by parchment; and with the tablets disappeared the old cylinder seals. Some of these seals still in use were very ancient: a shop in Nippur contained examples dating back more than a millennium to the Kassite era. The old religious rituals lingered on, and Babylonian deities, if often changed in character, were popular among many communities of western Asia. Babylonian law was widely used and scientific and astrological discoveries were studied. Further north, at Assur, a shrunken community of Assyrians survived. There they continued to worship their god Ashur and his consort, on the same spot as their ancestors had done before the disasters of 612 BC, although in a new temple. As late as AD 200–28, they were still using such grand old personal names as Sin-ahe-erba, even Esarhaddon, which pathetically recalled the vanished glories of the warrior nation.

Greek culture, carried across Asia by soldiers and settlers in the wake of Alexander and the Seleucids, came face to face with the cultures of Iran and Babylonia – and prevailed over neither. For a time, the Orientals picked out from Greek civilisation what they considered useful, especially for commerce: the calendar, names, administrative organisation, legal practices. Contracts at Dura and Avroman are composed in Greek, although all the parties involved may be Oriental. Plutarch even says that king Artavasdes of Armenia wrote Greek tragedies and histories, and many if not all the Arsacid monarchs could speak the language. Orientals continued to take Greek courtesy-names for use where Greek was being spoken and written and for other convenient purposes throughout the Parthian period. But the hearts of the Orientals remained untouched. Fundamentally, Greek culture remained a culture for Greeks. Where there were Greek settlers, there were gymnasia, baths and theatres; there were Greek constitutions and law, even literature and oratory. Iamblichus, the writer of Greek love stories, resided in Babylonia. The orator Amphicratus visited Seleucia, but when invited to remain and teach there, he replied insultingly that 'a dish would not contain a dolphin', and departed. The works of Greek writers in Parthia were utilised by Strabo, Trogus, Plutarch and others. Greek inscriptions in correct metre were engraved in honour of the god Apollo and an Iranian official, Zamaspes, at Susa. The two inscriptions to Zamaspes even have a poetic colouring of Doric Greek word forms: one is dated AD 1/2. But there is a surprising lack of articles and particles, and some of the terms and conceptions of the verses are Oriental. The letter of Artabanus III to Susa, dated December, AD 21, is in good Hellenistic Greek; but it is addressed to the officials and townsmen of *Susa*, the native name, whereas the Seleucid Greek name for the town had been Seleucia on the Eulaeus (river). On the other hand, the Greek on a rare coin issue of Gotarzes II (*c.* AD 38–51) has become ungrammatical, and the spelling of his name varies. At Dura Europos, the Greeks remained the upper stratum of local society throughout the Parthian occupation. Greek family organisation lasted there until at least 33/2 BC, and pure Macedonian Greek names were in use until a late period.

But everywhere, by the first century AD, the sun of Hellenism was setting. The Greeks remained in their towns, and their culture never deeply affected the main mass of the people outside. They tried to preserve their Greek blood, with diminishing success. They did not much object to mixed marriages, but if the offspring became Orientalized, these were then given the opprobrious name 'mixed Greek'. One by one, the citadels of

Hellenism fell. Susa was swallowed up by the kingdom of Elymais about AD 45 to re-emerge by AD 215 as fully Parthian. In AD 164–5, Dura was to be permanently taken and Seleucia on the Tigris devastated by the Romans. Greek inscriptions die away in the first half of the second century AD. Greek building forms, and the style and motifs of Greek art, as we shall see, had long been assimilated into 'Parthian' architecture and art. The inhabitants of Seleucia adopted the Babylonian custom of burying the dead within the floors and walls of their houses. By the later second century AD, little was left. The Greek legends of the Parthian royal coins were now barbarised beyond legibility – plainly, the die-cutters could no longer understand them. Perhaps it is not even too romantic to imagine the theatres closed and the gymnasia overgrown. Yet all was not lost, if much had been transmuted. The language survived: Greek was one of the three official languages of the inscriptions of the first Sasanian monarchs, and some communities continued resolutely to use the Seleucid calendar. Hellenism had put up a splendid fight in the east, even if the movement was doomed from the start, in the best tradition of Greek tragedy.

CHAPTER VI
Religion and Burial

THE ANCIENT RELIGION OF IRAN presents us with problems of every kind, largely because of an insufficient documentation. Reading between the lines of later texts, we can perhaps distinguish a primitive substratum of belief. 'Nature gods' were worshipped; maybe they fitted into an ideological framework which allotted their functions to the spheres of sovereignty, war and fecundity. Between the early religion of the Iranians and the Indians ideological connexions can be seen which must antedate the parting of these two Indo-European groups. Deities develop who personify the ideas embodied in their names, such as Mitra, god of the *mitra*, contract. Ethical qualities therefore become attached to these deities, known in Iran as the Ahuras. Into this world was born a prophet, Zarathushtra, or Zoroaster to the west. Tradition, combined with linguistic evidence, places his lifetime around 600 BC, and the area of his preaching as eastern Iran. Eventually, he found favour with the prehistoric king Vishtaspa. What was the content of his teaching?

Zoroastrianism is still a living faith, practised by a small minority in Iran and by the Parsees (or Persians) of India. From these groups portions of the sacred writings of antiquity, known collectively as the Avesta, have been recovered, together with ancient commentaries. To judge from important differences in language and conception, the sections of the Avesta must belong to periods ranging from perhaps Zoroaster's lifetime to the Sasanian epoch. Five groups of verses, the Gathas, stand out particularly because of the archaic language of their eastern Iranian dialect. They may well, therefore, belong to the prophet's own time, and their content reveals some of the fundamentals of his teaching. A new and personal relationship is estab-

lished between the worshipper and Zoroaster's supreme, universal deity, Ahura Mazda. Secondly, a basic dualism of Good
and Evil is conceived. These two principles are continually at
war, in both the spiritual and material worlds, but a day of
judgement will come when finally Good will triumph. Meanwhile, the war continues. Ahura Mazda (later Ohrmazd) is
assisted by other immortal powers in his struggle against the
evil spirit Angra Mainyu (later Ahriman) and his followers the
daivas, among whose ranks many of the old popular gods were
placed. The duty of man on earth is to strike blows against the
forces of Evil or Falsehood, and so to help in the establishment
of the kingdom of Mazda. Pious faith, the upholding of religious and moral truth, the promotion of beneficent works, particularly the cultivation of land – in these injunctions upon
man we see the ethical side of Zoroaster's message. Good
thoughts, good words and good deeds form the armour of
righteousness, as any Zoroastrian of today knows. The reward
for those who had upheld the Zoroastrian morality was an
immortality in paradise, while evil-doers were condemned to
endure punishment in the Dwelling of Falsehood.

Pure Zoroastrianism began as an enclave amidst the unreformed religion of Iran with its numerous deities, reverence for
the elements, and horse-sacrifice. Nevertheless, some of the basic
concepts, particularly those of the importance of Ahura Mazda
and the dualism of Good and Evil (or Arta, Rectitude, and
Druj, the Lie), became (or already were?) widespread. Striking
similarities in religious thought existed between Zoroaster and
the Achaemenid kings. Both prophet and monarchs worshipped
Ahura Mazda, and were therefore 'Mazdayasnians'. By the
end of the Achaemenid period, a considerable fusion had probably taken place between Zoroastrianism and the forms of worship administered by the priestly caste of the Magi. The long
history of the Magi began with their existence as a tribe, or
rather a special class, among the Medes who acted as priests of

unreformed Iranian religion. They always thought of themselves as belonging to one tribe, and were deeply concerned
with ritual. They soon became the priests for much of Iran.
Ultimately, when Zoroastrianism became the state religion of
the Sasanian Persians, the Magi were its spiritual leaders. How
far they had supported Zoroastrianism previously is a difficult
question, but some of them probably adopted and helped to
spread Zoroastrian ideas.

The more recent sections of the sacred book, the so-called
'Young Avesta', show notable differences from the prophet's
teaching in religious ideas and in the pantheon. Popular deities
are recognised beside those of the Gathas: Mithra, god of cove-
Plate 16   nants and of light; Anahita, goddess of waters and fertility;
Verethragna, god of war and victory; the Fravashis, protective
spirits. Later Zoroastrian religious law is given in the Vendi-
dad, the Anti-demonic Law, a compilation of rules and regu-
lations concerning ritual observances made perhaps by Magi.
Impurities and sins, together with penitences and means of
purification, are listed with levitical precision. For many of-
fences lashes of the whip, numbering from five to one thousand,
are prescribed. Sins include acts of violence and murder; and
pollution results from, for instance, the touching of corpses or
dead matter. The treatment of corpses is given special attention.
These must be exposed on *dakhmas* built of bricks – the so-called
'towers of silence' – for the flesh to be devoured by birds of
prey. Then the bare bones were to be placed in ossuaries. The
defilement of the elements earth and fire by inhumation or
cremation was absolutely forbidden. Water, too, was a sacred
element, and the worship of fire in particular became characteristic of later Zoroastrianism.

There is evidence of a general 'Mazdayasnian' religious climate in Seleucid and Parthian Iran, but little of the practice of
actual Zoroastrianism. The use at Nisa of Zoroastrian months,
and of names with a Zoroastrian ring such as '*hwrmzdyk*

(*Ohrmazdik) and *dynmzdk* (*Dinmazdak), may indicate a Zoroastrian atmosphere, but no proof of worship has been found. The Magi presumably continued to uphold throughout Iran various older and newer forms of worship, within the general 'Mazdayasnian' climate, of Ahura Mazda, the old Aryan gods, and developing Zoroastrianism. Certain traits of the 'Young Avesta' are already apparent in late Achaemenid inscriptions. Zoroastrianism was in all probability developing steadily towards its later Sasanian form throughout the Seleucid and Parthian periods, contributing to, and absorbing many elements from, Iranian religion. What struck Greek and Roman writers particularly in this era were curiosities of Iranian ritual. They noted the prominence of the worship of fire, the symbol of Ahura Mazda. In the city of Asaak, notes Isidorus, an everlasting fire was guarded. Sir Aurel Stein noticed large numbers of Parthian and Sasanian coins on a hillock at Maidan-i Naftun in the Iranian oil-fields: here jets of fire fed by perennially escaping natural gases must have attracted pilgrims. Presumably, as today, the holy temple fires were replenished with sweet-smelling wood. Priests wore a small veil tied around the face when they approached them, to prevent their breath from polluting the sacred element. Water also was holy. Justin remarks upon the Parthian reverence for rivers. When Tiridates, Arsacid king of Armenia and a Magus as well, travelled to Rome to receive his crown from Nero, he went by land to avoid pollution of the sea. A bundle of rods, the *barsom*, entered into religious ritual, and the priests must also have drunk the intoxicating liquor *haoma*. This was prepared from a herb, regarded as divine and known to Plutarch as *omomi*, by a long, elaborate process, to provide the priestly communion drink. This plant is the *soma* of the Indians, and therefore its worship must be extremely ancient, although it is not mentioned in the Gathas. The exposure of corpses was a widespread practice. When Alexander the Great reached Bactria, he found that the villagers and townsfolk flung corpses into the street and left them there. Justin says explicitly that 'dead bodies are generally exposed to be devoured by birds or dogs. The bare bones are then covered with earth.' Strabo adds that these dogs had a special name, Grave-makers.

Various types of debased Mazda worship, often heavily influenced by the Chaldean astrology of Babylonia, penetrated the Roman east. Some of these influences were historically insignificant. The Magi claimed to possess all kinds of recondite and occult knowledge. Wonderful powers, for instance, were ascribed by them to plants. This usually ludicrous information was kept in books, and earned the contempt of Pliny. Necromancy was another of their specialities. The philosopher Menippus, according to Lucian, wished to visit the underworld to ask the seer Tiresias for his opinion on the best life. He therefore contacted a Magus in Babylonia. The grotesque initiation prescribed by the Magus, the vegetarian diet, strange rites, flaming torch and bellowed gibberish, we learn, had the desired effect. From such practices arose the association between Magi and magic. Other influences, however, were of the greatest importance in the development of thought. Basic concepts of Iranian religion, the dualism, the duty of man, the universality of God, the last judgement and the existence of paradise, all entered into the common stock of western Asian ideas, drawn as a whole from several Oriental traditions and from Greek philosophy. These influences helped to produce a whole crop of related philosophical and religious movements, including the mystery and saviour cults. From the kind of Mazda worship prevalent in Asia Minor emerged Mithraism, the mystery cult of the god Mithra considered as the god of the sun. This cult became widespread in the Roman Empire, especially among the military and mercantile communities, and Mithraists adopted the old Iranian idea that the Good and Evil Spirits were twin brothers, the sons of Zurvan, Infinite Time. From a combination of western Asiatic, and partly Iranian, ideas with Christianity arose a number of Gnostic systems, and an important Gnostic sect, that of the Mandeans, was established in western Parthia. Among this welter of Mazdayasnian, Zoroastrian and related beliefs, what was the religion of the Arsacids and the Parni?

Again, a lack of documentation makes this a difficult question to answer. They may at first have brought in some divinities of the nomads. The king was allegedly 'Brother of the Sun and Moon', which are indeed represented on some Parthian coins. Several more or less fragmentary statues, some of them greater than life-size, were found at Nisa, Shami and elsewhere. When taken with the reliefs of Nemrud Dagh in Commagene (*c.* 69–34 BC), on which kings of the present and past are shown, these discoveries may indicate a fairly widespread cult of the deified monarch or ancestor from an early period. The beardless archer, shown seated on the reverse of most Parthian silver coins, probably has some religious significance – but does it represent the deified Arsaces, some Parni god, or a resuscitation in Parthian guise of the archer of Achaemenid coins? Once established, the Arsacids never adopted full Zoroastrianism. The Sasanians would not recognise them as true believers. But they do seem to have embraced ordinary Mazda worship, probably from political motives more than anything, so as to conciliate the main mass of their subjects. The Magi were respected by the king. They attended the second Council of State, and allegedly frequented the palace of Vardanes at Babylon. Royal names beginning with Arta- and Mithra- indicate an awareness of the religion. The Arsacid Tiridates, ruler of Armenia, observed Magian ritual. In a Greek inscription of Susa, the 'daimon' (that is, the *fravashi* or guardian spirit) of king Phraates (V?) is honoured. Furthermore, Isidorus' remark that an eternal fire burned at Asaak where 'Arsaces' was crowned, taken together with a seal from Nisa, suggests that each Arsacid had a royal fire burning continually for him, a custom of their

Plate 6e

Plates 47, 48, 51

Plate 30

Plate 6

Sasanian (and Zoroastrian) successors. According to Parsee tradition, one Arsacid monarch at least performed a great service for Zoroastrianism. The original twenty-one books in which what had been revealed to the prophet was recorded were mostly burnt by 'Iskander the Rumi' (Alexander the Great). The collection of the surviving fragments was allegedly begun by king Valakhsh or Vologases (I?). Ardashir Papakan (*c*. AD 224–40), the first Sasanian monarch, proclaimed this faith the state religion and the Avesta its holy writ, and the final purification of the corpus was completed under his successors. But to the Sasanians, it was Ardashir, and no Arsacid, who had saved Zoroastrianism. The Arsacid kings, after all, had been buried in tombs, at first in Nisa and later supposedly in Arbela: their corpses were not exposed. Furthermore, Greek deities in abundance are shown on Parthian coins – Victory, Tyche, Zeus, Artemis and so on. Lastly, we hear of no religious persecutions under the Arsacids, who seem to have been concerned with the political aspects of religion alone.

Plates 17, 20 Arsacid tolerance allowed many religions to flourish unfettered within their empire. Innumerable figurines, found mostly in western Iran and made in Greek and Oriental styles, represent a variety of deities, and constituted cheap religious dedications as proof of piety. In Babylonia, hymns in Sumerian, a language unspoken for two millennia, were still studied. Babylonian religion and ritual lived on not only in its home terrain but also over a broad region of western Parthia and Roman Syria. In spite of political eclipse, the Babylonian priesthoods preserved their intellectual domination. Bel, the title of Babylonian Marduk, became a god in his own right in some communities. The goddess Ishtar continued to be worshipped well into our era. Nanai, of Sumerian origin, was widely revered and possessed a temple and estate at Nisa. Both goddesses had fertility aspects, and their worship involved such repulsive practices as temple prostitution. Babylonian influence also produced characteristic

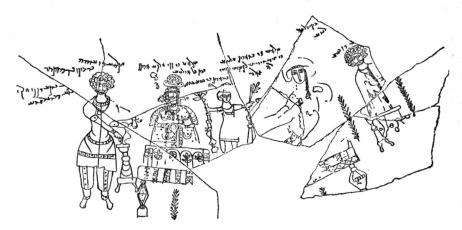

groupings of deities into pairs and triads. At Palmyra, Aglibol the moon god was a member of two separate triads, which must have caused confusion among his followers. Perhaps the most pervasive of Babylonian influences was, unfortunately, that of astrology. Men came from afar to study this rich store of observations, amassed over millennia and designed to make known the ways of Fate to man. The term 'Chaldean' even became a title of honour.

Over western Parthia as a whole, an entire galaxy of Semitic divinities and beliefs is in evidence. There were primitive cults of high places, of waters, rivers, lakes, wells and the sea; cults of trees, and cults of stones, especially those called by the Greeks *baetyla*. These, as their name suggests – *beth-el*, the house of god – were regarded as objects into which the deity incorporated himself. Then, on a higher plane, there were divinities of every kind, Aramaic, Arabic, Phoenician and so on, who produced fertility, good crops and rainfall, and were often armed to protect their adherents. In northern Mesopotamia, Assyrian

Fig. 20

Plates 21, 33, 67, 68

Fig. 21

Fig. 22

cults survived. Pilgrims also travelled from Babylonia to worship the Lady of Hierapolis-Bambyce in northern Syria, Lucian tells us. Religious ritual was often complex and involved processions: the simplest rite, and that most often represented in art, consisted of the casting of incense upon a burner. Many a temple of this region, as we shall discover, was decorated internally with wall-paintings, arranged in superimposed tiers. A notable feature of Semitic religion was the local character of many divinities. Every area had its *baal* and *baalat*, its Lord and Lady or protective deities, and many a village boasted its *gny* (genie) or guardian spirit. This localism is in complete contrast with the universality of Ahura Mazda.

Greek religion, like Greek culture in general, was largely confined to the Hellenic community. Hymns to Apollo were engraved at Susa; Greek deities appear on Arsacid coins and

Fig. 21   Relief of a Parthian dignitary throwing incense from a vessel on to a burner, carved on an isolated rock at Behistun/Bisutun. Probably second century AD.

Fig. 22   Painted decoration on the interior walls of the cult-room of the temple of Zeus Theos, Dura Europos. Second century AD. *(After M. Rostovtzeff,* Dura Europos and its Art, *pl. 13)*

seals; statuettes of Zeus, Heracles, Athena, Aphrodite and so on have been found. But whenever Greek deities are represented or invoked, we must ask whether they may not be Oriental deities in disguise. For the arrival of Hellenism in the east sparked off an immense new religious movement – the syncretism of Greek and Oriental deities. Henceforth, Semitic (including Babylonian), Iranian and Greek deities began to be considered identical. Thus Ahura Mazda became the Iranian equivalent of Bel, Mithra of Shamash, and Anahita of Ishtar or Nanai. Apollo in the Susan hymn is addressed as Mara, a Syrian title, 'Lord'. Heracles was usually the Hellenic aspect of the Semitic Nergal

Fig. 3

Plate 19

or the Iranian Verethragna, and Athena of the Arab goddess Allat. But the most striking example of all lies in the syncretism of gods present in the dedications of the statues which still guard the colossal tomb of king Antiochus I of Commagene (69–34 BC). The chief statue represents Zeus-Oromasdes (Ohrmazd, a later form of Ahura Mazda); a second Apollo-Mithras-Helios-Hermes; and a third, Artagnes (Verethragna)-Heracles-Ares. A further stage in this movement began in Hellenistic Syria and Babylonia, in which all gods and goddesses tended to be welded into one omnipotent, universal and ineffable deity whose most splendid manifestation is the Sun. But the history of this solar syncretism belongs more to the Roman west than to Parthia.

Plates 29, 31

Other religions practised in Parthia are still familiar today. Ever since their deportation to Babylonia and Mesopotamia by Nebuchadnezzar, Jews had flourished and multiplied in those regions. They regarded the Arsacids as well disposed, and proselytised without hindrance. Indeed, a vassal monarch, Izates II of Adiabene, even became a Jew. As for Christians, evidence is scanty indeed. They had become widespread throughout the Roman east during the first century AD, and by about AD 200 there seem to have been Christian communities at Arbela, Kirkuk and elsewhere east of the Tigris. The Christian writer Tatianus was born in Parthia. Traditionally, an early Council of the Church was held at Edessa, capital of Osroene, in AD 198, to settle the date of Easter. Buddhism penetrated the eastern Iranian regions in the Hellenistic period, when the Indian king Asoka embraced it around 260 BC and sent missionaries into Bactria. The Greek king Agathocles, reigning in eastern Iran about 180–165 BC, had a Buddhist stupa depicted on his coins. In this same century a deep schism split the Buddhists into two persuasions. Those of the Hinayana, or 'Lesser Vehicle', continued to adhere strictly to their founder's doctrine. Buddhists of the Mahayana or 'Greater

Vehicle', however, mixed these doctrines with ideas and popular beliefs from other Indians cults. The latter persuasion spread northward into central Asia, and was included among the cults adopted by Kanishka, ruler of the Kushan empire to the east of Parthia in the second century AD. He held a council to fix the principles of the Mahayana and to revise its canon. Two great statues of Buddha more than 100 feet high, carved in a lofty cliff face of the Hindu Kush at Bamiyan in Afghanistan, survive as a monumental memorial of his enthusiasm. Astonishing by their size and remarkable in their preservation, they overawe the indefatigable traveller who can get to see them. But, by a strange quirk of history, it was no Kushan who first translated the Buddhist scriptures for the distant Chinese, but, traditionally, an Arsacid prince of this period who was living in China.

By a further strange turn of fate, we learn from an inscription of Palmyra that in Vologasias of all places, the Parthian commercial city of Babylonia, there stood a temple of the deified Roman emperors, the Augusti!

Burial customs can illuminate further the religions of Parthia. Exposure of corpses was practised by Mazda worshippers, and the Young Avesta prescribes that when the bodies of the deceased have been exposed, the bones are to be gathered together and placed in *astodans*, ossuaries. This type of burial was indeed in vogue in the eastern part of the Empire. Ossuaries of terracotta, usually unglazed and handmoulded, have come to light at Nisa, and in Sogdiane from the later Parthian period. But throughout the towns of the western Parthian regions, inhumation of various kinds was customary. In its simplest form, it consisted simply of the burial of the corpse within the walls or floors of mudbrick houses. This was an old Babylonian custom, still widely in use in spite of its hygienic drawbacks. Other methods of inhumation varied from the humblest to the grandiose. Bodies, especially those of children, might be crammed into a jar or covered with a large pot. In other cases, coffins of a few standard types were used. Sometimes the dead were laid out-side the houses in wooden or terracotta coffins, within a little tomb built of tiles or bricks which might boast a vaulted top. Such tiny vaults often contain only one or a few burials. But more elaborate examples, such as those excavated at Seleucia, take on the appearance of family vaults. Set beneath the earth and roofed with a barrel vault of bricks, vault 131, for instance, was divided inside into *loculi* or recesses. It was approached down a steep staircase, and was periodically reopened to receive fresh burials. The terracotta sarcophagi used in these burials are principally of two types, known irreverently as the 'bath-tub' and 'slipper' varieties. The 'bath-tubs' were inherited by the Parthians from the Assyrians; a cover was normally added, and the whole often glazed and richly decorated. The 'slipper' sar-cophagi were in use from the first century BC onwards. As their name suggests, they resemble a slipper or shoe in shape, with a more or less oval opening at the wider end. This was closed with a fitted cover or filled in with bricks. A small hole at the tapering end allowed the escape of the chemicals of decay. Many of these sarcophagi bear a green or bue glaze and an elab-orate decoration. The sides and top are most often divided up

Plate 22

into rectangular compartments, in each of which appears a re-peated figure – usually a soldier, nude goddess or dancer. Both the shape and the decoration in 'compartments' seem to have been borrowed from the mummies of Egypt with their orna-mentally bound wrappings. Even more clearly of Egyptian inspiration are some anthropoid sarcophagi found at Babylon and Susa. With the bodies were buried objects of all kinds. Pottery, glassware, vessels of stone and metal, weapons, jewel-lery, figurines and various articles of daily use – bronze mir-ors, ivory combs, lamps – have all turned up. At Babylon, a diadem or wreath of leaves of gold, or a crown of real olive-leaves, was sometimes laid on the forehead of the deceased. The inhabitants of Seleucia were also buried with amulets and

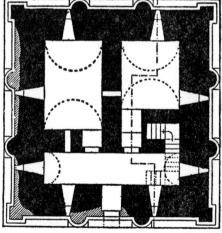

*Fig. 23 Plan and restored elevation of tomb YI,
Hatra, second century AD. (After W. Andrae.
Hatra (II), 1912, fig. 126)*

models of keys, and coins were often placed in the corpse's mouth or palm – so that the dead could pay their fee to Charon for transport to the Underworld? The fact that food and drink, and figurines of women to act as conjugal companions in the next world, were found with the burials of Seleucia shows clearly that these people believed that life after death was not just a shadowy or spiritual existence, but would bring actual physical enjoyment.

The upper classes of Parthian society were buried in far greater state. The royal tombs of Nisa and Arbela still lie undiscovered. But in the mound of New Nisa the remnants of an imposing brick mausoleum, perhaps in use for the nobility, were found. A row of columns with 'aboriginal Ionic' capitals fronted a proud portico. The upper part of the mausoleum façade was crowned with the old Assyrian decoration of stepped crenellations, as were many Parthian buildings. Inside, there was a square central chamber surrounded by a corridor, perhaps a shrine. A number of rooms and passages contained *loculi,* long and narrow recesses for sarcophagi. The buildings seem to belong to the second century BC. *Loculi,* therefore, constitute a feature of tombs throughout the Parthian Empire. They form an integral part of a whole series of attractive mausolea of brick and stone erected in the western Parthian cultural area. At Hatra, rectangular stone buildings of the later Parthian period, now mostly more or less ruined, were built to house the mercantile and princely dead both outside and inside the city walls, as was the regular Mesopotamian custom. The exteriors were frequently clothed in a Romanised decoration of engaged columns, pilasters and entablatures. Within, there were often two storeys of chambers joined by a staircase and roofed with simple stone vaults. Narrow windows illuminated the interiors. Pale imitations in brick of the Hatrene mausolea stood in nearby Assur, again with vaulted chambers. But by far the most singular and striking tombs of the Parthian area were the towers

Fig. 2

Fig. 23

Plate 26

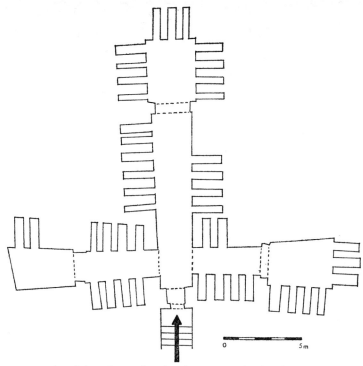

Fig. 24 Plan of the underground tomb or hypogeum *of Lishamsh, Palmyra, in the form reached in the third century* AD. *After H. Ingholt, Berytus V, 1938, pl. XXXIX*

erected notably at Dura and Palmyra mostly during the first three centuries AD. The funerary tower immediately evokes the Zoroastrian 'towers of silence', but no connexion can be found. At both Palmyra and Dura, the tower was but one of several forms of funerary building. The *hypogeum* or subterranean family mausoleum, the tomb-temple and even the tomb-house constituted further varieties. At Palmyra the tower and *hypogeum* were sometimes combined. Each tomb seems originally to have belonged to one family, and contained numerous *loculi* for the insertion of sarcophagi. But whereas the *loculi* of the Dura towers faced outwards, those of Palmyra opened on internal halls. The impressive stone towers of Palmyra, the 'houses of eternity'

Fig. 24

as the Palmyrenes called them, are justifiably famous, not only for their often almost perfectly preserved façades, but also for the richness of their interior decoration. Each coffin-recess was normally closed by a stone sculpted bust which 'represented' the deceased, or else the ends of a group of coffins would be shut off by a larger sculpture. These reliefs have mostly been stripped from their rightful positions for public and private art collections. The sarcophagi are gone, and the mummies that lay within them were used for purposes of magic by the Arabs, who left behind just a few shreds of the costly clothing from ancient China, India and elsewhere in which the bodies had been wrapped. But much of the decoration remains: stone or stucco architecture and paintings brighten the funerary chambers. This display, and the fact that, as many inscriptions reveal, the business instincts of the Palmyrene merchants prompted them to hire and sell *loculi* within the family tomb to less fortunate outsiders, provide ammunition for the moralist. Even the largest and most splendid of these tombs, however, is utterly dwarfed by the last resting place of king Antiochus I of Commagene at Nemrud Dagh. A huge artificial mound covers the grave and broad terraces surround it. But we are now fully in the realm of architecture, and to this we must turn next.

Plate 37

Plate 29

CHAPTER VII

Architecture

EARTHQUAKES APART, the local conditions and climate of Parthia favoured the long life of even comparatively
flimsy structures. The warm, dry weather enabled the inhabitants of western Asia to build most commonly in simple, sun-
dried mud brick, as today. The parts of these buildings most
likely to suffer from the action of water or from the feet and
shoulders of the inhabitants, the foundations, jambs and corners,
could be constructed in the far more durable if more expensive
kiln-baked brick, or else in stone if that was available. Fired
brick was also used for the whole of certain important buildings,
such as the palaces of local governors and temples. Stone was
used only when there was a plentiful local supply and when
economic conditions allowed, as at Hatra. Wood was, in general, scarce throughout western Asia. It often had to be brought
from great distances; consequently it was expensive and used as
little as possible. Strabo, writing in the early first century AD,
says that the people of Mesopotamia would erect brick vaults to
roof the rooms of their houses rather than use wooden beams.
Not for nothing did the cedar forests of Lebanon earn their
ancient fame.

The enormous extent of the Parthian Empire and the different traditions of the regions which it embraced must warn us
against expecting any great uniformity in Parthian architecture.
Moreover, the lack of wide excavation in Iran itself has meant
that far too little is known of the buildings of the central part
of the Empire. But in spite of this, some important elements and
and types of building occur, particularly from the turn of our
era onwards, which supersede older local characteristics across
or over large portions of the Empire and which therefore have a
good claim to be called Parthian.

The Parthian domains came to include many towns of extreme antiquity, such as Babylon or Uruk (the Biblical Erech). Some of these, Assur for example, flourished once again after a bad period. Others were now little more than villages, nestling amidst the gargantuan remnants of ancient splendour. Others again, like Kalakh (Nimrud) had been moved from their original site, which had grown into a *tell* or mound too high for convenient living. The planning of these ancient towns had sometimes in the past attained considerable orderliness, but always tended to lapse into a haphazard sprawl, especially in periods of depression. Secondly, there were the Hellenistic cities of western Asia, laid out in the usual Greek 'Hippodamian' manner, with a basically rectangular plan and with streets crossing at right angles. In this way hundreds of equal units of land were easily divided up and shared out democratically between the citizens.

For a number of Parthian cities a different plan was adopted, more or less circular in shape. This is true both of new foundations such as Ctesiphon or Hatra, and of the enlargements of *Fig. 25* such older towns as Merv. The idea of the circular plan may

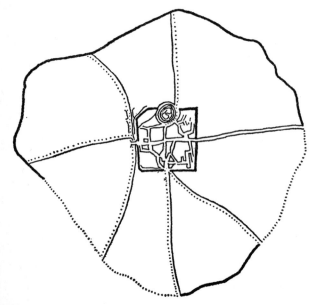

Fig. 25 Plan of the city of Merv in the Parthian period, showing the ractangular layout of the Seleucid town of Antioch in the centre. (After Vestnik Drevnei Istorii, *1951, 4, fig. 1)*

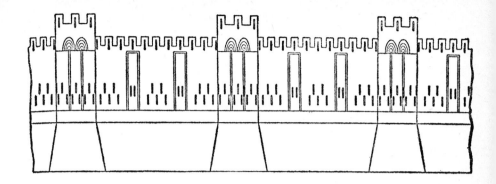

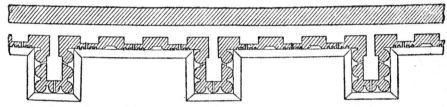

Fig. 26   Plan and elevation of the Parthian city walls of Merv (after Vestnik Drevnei Istorii, 1951, 4, fig. 6)

Plate 18

have grown from the roughly circular shape of Assyrian mili‑
tary camps. A circular enclosure is not only easier to defend
than a rectangle, but the space within can be enclosed with
considerably less walling than that required for the equivalent
area of a rectangle. The circular plan lived on into the Sasanian
and Islamic periods. It was usual for Parthian towns to be wall‑
ed, a sobering reminder of contemporary conditions. The walls
of Merv were of mud brick, with towers, step‑shaped battlements Fig. 26
and numerous arrow‑slits; they resemble certain Assyrian
town defences. The walls of Hatra were basically of stone, and
doubled. With their many towers and few gateways, these de‑
fences defeated Roman siege attempts more than once.

   Within the Parthian city, the most important buildings were
normally the palace (the centre of administration) and the tem‑
ples. Prominent also must have been the bazaar areas, like the

Oriental *sukh* discovered at Dura Europos. The ordinary houses were usually built around a courtyard, especially in western Parthia, where the Babylonian type of house was widespread, even in towns originally Greek such as Dura. Usually with one storey only, sometimes partly with two, these houses surrounded the court, and the main group of rooms was placed on the southern side. The roof, always flat, was reached by a *Fig. 16* staircase normally set in one corner of the court. The first storey and roof were in constant use for eating and sleeping, and probably provided a welcome escape from the odours of the ground floor, where the cooking and sanitary arrangements were situated. The latter were primitive indeed; the entirely inadequate drainage, when combined with the hot weather, nurtured disease. In Babylon gardens, or patches of waste land, often lay between the straggling dwellings of this period. The domestic buildings of Assur, which now prospered again, show some innovations in the old scheme. Strabo had noted that rooms in the houses of western Parthia were often vaulted, although post-and-lintel construction in which some wood was employed must also have been normal practice. In the latest Parthian period at Assur (the early third century AD), a special open-fronted room, roofed with a barrel vault and facing north on to the interior court, began to be included in the houses. This is the *iwan* (the modern term), a striking new feature of Parthian architecture which, as we shall shortly see, had already appeared in larger buildings.

On many Parthian sites buildings have been discovered which, from their size and complexity, must have been palaces. Here the local governor or ruler would have resided. A Hellenistic example was found at ancient Nippur in Babylonia. The plan, with a peristyle court, was Greek; so too were the architectural features, but it was all built in the local materials, baked brick and stucco. The earliest known Parthian palace included Hellenistic forms. This, the 'royal palace' of Old

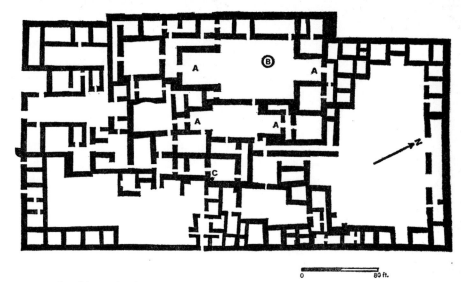

Fig. 27   Plan of the Parthian 'palace' of Seleucia on the Tigris, showing iwans (A), pool (B) and well (C), second century AD. (After L. Waterman, Preliminary Report upon the Excavations at Tel Umar, Iraq, fig. 7)

Nisa, erected during the first century of Parthian rule, was constructed in the local medium of sun-dried brick. A colonnaded
open terrace and a square central hall with unusual columns   Plate 3
which underwent several alterations were luxurious features.
The façade decorations included metopes, a frieze and further
items from the Hellenistic repertoire of decoration together with
others more Iranian in content; they were rendered in terracotta.
But elements of plan and decoration which are distinctive
enough to be called Parthian do not seem to appear in palaces
until the first century AD. Their arrival can be closely followed
in the 'palace' of Seleucia. This enormous dwelling was built   Fig. 27
around a series of courts, on to which opened rooms and
Hellenistic 'megaron' halls, with columns placed before the
entrance of each hall. Concessions to local practice meant that
the megaron halls faced north instead of south, that there was
no peristyle, and that probably all roofs were flat, but the plan is

still recognisably Greek. The palace was rebuilt at the time of the revolt of Seleucia, which ended around AD 42, and emerged with fundamental differences. The column was no longer a structural element. From now on, it became simply an orna/ment, rendered in gypsum plaster and engaged on walls to di/vide them into decorative panels. Equally surprising is the con/version of almost all the megaron halls into a new type of hall: the open/fronted and usually barrel/vaulted *iwan*. In the final period, the palace walls were thickened to carry further vaults on high arches.

The early history of the *iwan* is far from clear. It became a standard feature of later Iranian architecture and seems always to have been at home in the country. A building at Nisa, the 'Square House' south of the 'palace', contained four *iwans* which opened on to a central court. These may be earlier than the more definitely dated examples of Mesopotamia. If so, then the *iwan* may fairly be claimed as 'Parthian'. But its early hist/ory remains obscure. Some would derive it from the open room with a loggia, the so/called *hilani* of many near/eastern palaces of the earlier first millennium BC. Others see it as a 'stone tent', the natural architectural product of a recently nomadic people who wished, even when settled, to remain in contact with the open air. This contact is certainly achieved in a room with only three walls. But neither theory seems fully to account for the frequent grouping of the *iwans*, either side by side or around the court, or for the customary vaulting of the roof. Moreover, the use of the *iwan* was not confined to secular architecture. Per/haps the unexcavated cities of Iran hold the key to this problem.

Certainly the use of the *iwan* was not unusual in eastern Iran by the first century AD, for *iwan* halls are present in the vast 'royal palace' of that period at Kuh/i Khwaja, splendidly situat/ed on an island in the centre of the Hamun lake, Seistan. The rooms of the palace, built of sun/dried brick, surround an enormous rectangular court. From the entrance on the south, one

Fig. 28

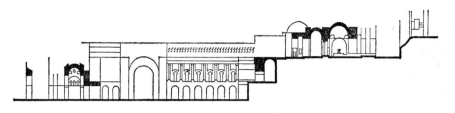

→N

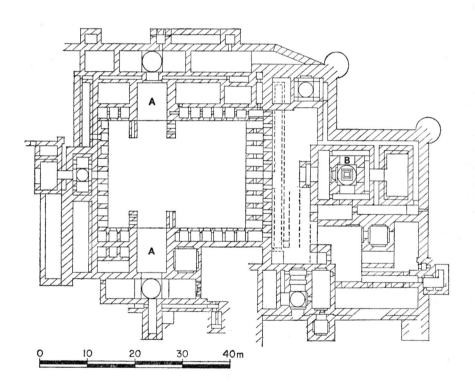

0   10   20   30   40m

Fig. 28   Plan and section of the main building of the 'palace' at Kuh-i Khwaja, Seistan, probably first century AD. *A* Iwans, *B fire temple. (After E. Herzfeld,* Iran in the Ancient East, *plate XCVII)*

Fig. 29

entered the main court of the palace to find a huge vaulted *iwan* to right and left. Continuing northwards and uphill, one passed through the northern section of the palace, across a gallery decorated with a remarkable series of wall-paintings, up to the platform where stood the fire temple which crowned the whole ensemble. Impressive examples of the fully developed iwan were also found in the Parthian palace of Assur. Here, before AD 100, a complex of rooms, which included two opposed *iwans*, was arranged around a main court that did not quite manage to be rectangular. Additional courts, including a peri-

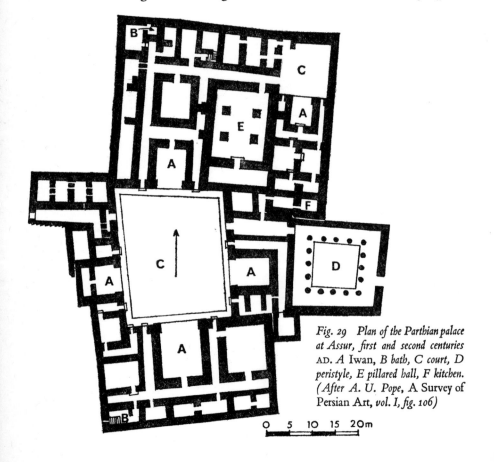

Fig. 29   Plan of the Parthian palace at Assur, first and second centuries AD. A Iwan, B bath, C court, D peristyle, E pillared hall, F kitchen. (After A. U. Pope, A Survey of Persian Art, vol. I, fig. 106)

0   5   10   15   20m

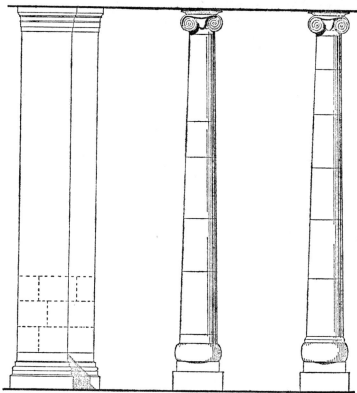

Fig. 30   Ionic columns and antae of the Seleucid/Parthian temple at Khurha. (After E
Herzfeld, Iran in the Ancient East, fig. 383)

style court misused as a vestibule, were also present. During the
second century AD, two more *iwans* were added to the main
court. Their façades were covered with a remarkable decoration
in coloured stucco of half-columns, arches and friezes that reduced the area of plane surface to a minimum. Yellow, red,
green, brown and blue were used with zest. The palace came
to a sorry end, probably during Severus' eastern campaign of
AD 198, and a rash of mean houses spread over its ruins.

Plate 27

The religious architecture of the Empire was not as diverse as
were the cults. There is little sign of architectural innovation

during the first couple of centuries of Parthian rule. Older traditions retained their stranglehold, and their effects often lasted
into our era. In 170 BC, the Anu-Antum temple in Uruk was
raised in the ancient Babylonian style. Greek tradition produced

Fig. 30
the colossal, if aberrant, sanctuaries of Khurha and Kangavar
in western Iran. Here a huge rectangular court was walled
off, the walls were lined with columns on the interior, and in
the centre of the court stood a temple of basically Greek plan,
complete with peristyle and columned entrance. The maltreat-
ment of Greek forms by the builders of these sanctuaries has
provoked much amusement among classical archaeologists. At
Khurha, the builders used strangely elongated stone columns,
with bulging Oriental bases, smooth shafts and an unclassical
ratio between base diameter and height of 1:11. The capitals
are of the 'aboriginal Ionic' variety, that is, of the Asiatic form
already in use before the Greeks developed their Ionic capital

Fig. 31
from it. The sanctuary of Kangavar is mentioned (as Concobar)
by Isidorus of Charax, who attributes it to the goddess Artemis,
or, in Iranian terms, Anahita. The stonework reflects Achaemenid tradition. The architectural forms include columns with
Doric capitals crowned by a Corinthian abacus and set on unusual Ionic bases. Along the top of the foundation stonework
runs a gargantuan *cyma* moulding. The classical forms and orders
are here so distorted that it is very difficult to date the ensembles
by analogy, but they seem to belong to the last couple of centuries BC. Strangely enough, the architecture of Kangavar has a
certain elegance about it.

By the first century AD we find that the Parthian architects
have absorbed a repertoire of these classical forms and transformed them into something rich and strange, in which older and
newer Oriental forms also play an important role. Several tem-

Fig. 32(A)
ples of this later period have been excavated in the Mesopotamian region. A tiny Parthian brick chapel at Uruk, huddled up
against the enormous walls of the Anu-Antum temple, carries

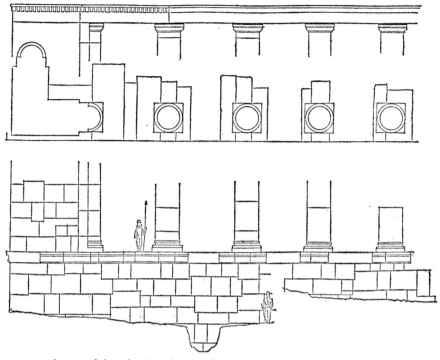

Fig. 31   Elevation of the Seleucid/Parthian temple at Kangavar, perhaps originally built around 200 BC. (After E. Herzfeld, Iran in the Ancient East, fig. 380)

on the outside a system of decoration which immediately marks it as belonging to this period. A series of half-columns attached to the outer façade divides it into panels, in each of which there is an arched recess. A very similar decoration was carved on the stone walls of the sanctuary of Istakhr, near Persepolis. The capitals of the half-columns here were intended to be of the Corinthian order. The prominent use of this order, and the crowning of the recess between each pair of engaged columns with a conch-shell motif, would seem by analogies with Roman architecture to place this temple in the first two centuries AD. A more complicated version of this wall decoration diversified the outside of another Parthian temple at Uruk, that of the

Fig. 32(B)   god Gareus. Internally, the brick temple possesses the fore-cella, cult-room and cult-niches of the ancient Babylonian temple.
Fig. 33   Outside, however, modern influence from the Roman Mediterranean is paramount. Half-columns, with Attic bases, Ionic capitals (of a sort) and Doric fluting, punctuate the façade and enclose recesses in each of which a blind arch rises on pilasters. Above the entablature lies an attic storey. Each façade looks something like a triple Roman triumphal arch. But a Roman would have been puzzled by the decorative reliefs of burnt clay, representing dogs and winged dragons with long tails, which constituted further decoration. The whole temple was coated, for the protection of the brickwork, with gypsum stucco. This must have given it an appearance of brilliant whiteness. An inscription found near by identifies the temple, which was standing by AD 110.

Fig. 32   Plans of temples of the Parthian period (after C. Hopkins, Berytus 1942, figs. 1, 2, 3, 9)
(A) Chapel in the Anu-Antum precinct, Uruk, first or second century AD. *(B)* Temple of Gareus, Uruk, built before AD 110. *(C)* The Peripteros of Assur, later Parthian period. *(D)* The Iranian temple of Taxila, Scytho-Parthian period

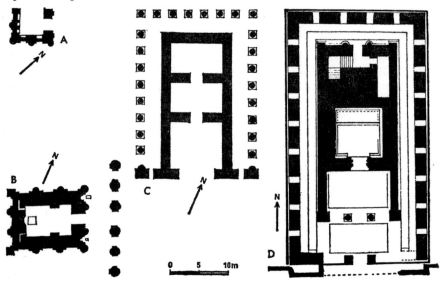

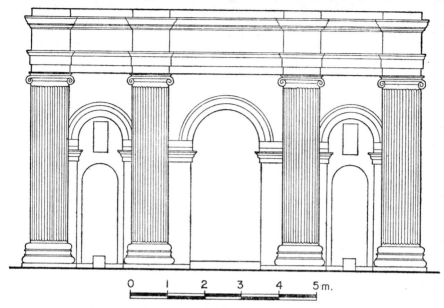

Fig. 33 Façade of the temple of Gareus, Uruk, built before AD *110. (After E. Heinrich,* Abhandlungen *der Preussischen Akademie, 1935, pl. 13a)*

The bases of six columns, once linked together by arches, were discovered some way in front of the Gareus temple. Perhaps a covered arcade encircled the sacred area, which was probably bounded by a wall. A similar arcade on columns surrounded the curious temple at Assur dubbed the Peripteros Building. This arcade is, however, joined to the temple to form a peristyle. Here the columns, normally engaged in Parthian work, have therefore retained their true function. At least three traditions are discernible in its architecture. The internal arrangement, with *pronaos* (vestibule) and *naos* (cult-room), is firmly derived from Assyrian and Babylonian precedent. The appearance of the outer arcade would not have shocked a visiting Roman unduly. But the additional outer cult-room, which with its arched entrance resembles a Parthian *iwan*, and the stuccoed decoration of the front façade, recall the Assur palace

Fig. 32(C)

127

architecture. Oriental traditions also determined the plans of most of the brick Parthian sanctuaries at Dura Europos. These were built around a large open court. On the side opposite the entrance stood the cult chapel or chapels, and around the court rose rooms and chapels set up by religious societies. One curi-ous feature of some of these temples is the addition of a small theatre. The temple of Atargatis, for instance, boasts two, and the discovery of a little theatre adjoining the porch of an open-air temple at Seleucia confirms the impression that it was a lo-cal phenomenon, designed to enable groups of spectators to witness certain rites.

The latter temple seems to be an example of an open-air Iranian type, as opposed to those planned on Babylonian or Greek lines. It consisted simply of a court, built before about AD 120, and surrounded by a wall. The outer side of the wall was plain, but on the inside the usual engaged half-columns linked by arches relieved the plain surface. A covered corridor also ran round the inside of the boundary wall. In Iran, several open sanctuaries are known. One, at Bard-i Nishandeh, was in use for centuries. Another, largely open to the skies, once stood at Shami in the Bakhtiari mountains of western Iran. Here again the walls were lined by a colonnade. The discovery of statues and religious bric-à-brac that ranged in date from the mid-Hellenistic period to probably the first century AD seems to assign the sanctuary originally to the Seleucid era. There was perhaps another such enclosure, in which fire worship could have been practised, at Takht-i Sulaiman in north-west-ern Iran. This site became an important centre for religious pil-grimage and worship immediately after the fall of the Arsacids, and so the spot was probably already regarded as holy in the Parthian period.

Plate 18

The *iwan* made its début in religious architecture as well as in palaces during the first century AD. At Assur, as on other ancient sites, temples continued to rise on holy ground. The

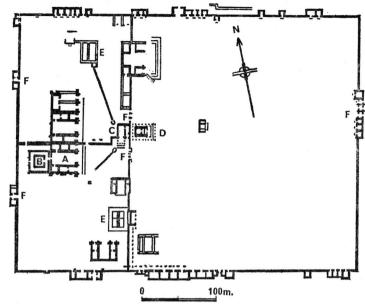

Fig. 34   Plan of the Sanctuary of the Sun. Hatra, first and second centuries AD (after W. Andrae, Hatra (II), 1912, pl. III)
(A) Great South Iwan (B) Sanctuary of Shamash (C) Temple of Shahru (D) 'Hel-lenistic' temple (E) Cistern (F) Gate

pair of juxtaposed *iwans* which were erected over the old Ashur temple were very probably used for religious purposes. In the second century AD, a third *iwan* was added and the court graced with gateways, the whole rendered in sun-dried brick and covered with gypsum plaster.

The colossal sanctuary of the Sun God which rose in the centre of the desert city of Hatra (el-Hadr) had a similar life-history. The chief temple began in a modest way as two juxta-posed groups of brick *iwans*. But by AD 77 limestone had begun to replace the humbler material. The change occurred perhaps through the impact of Roman ideas. The brick *iwans* became tall barrel-vaulted halls, set side by side in two groups of three. In each group, a small *iwan*, with an upper room

Plate 23

129

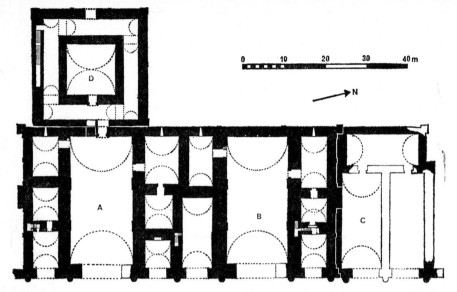

Fig. 35 Plan of the main temples (D Shrine of Shamash) and iwans *(A–C) of the Sanctuary of the Sun, Hatra, later first and second centuries* AD *(after A. U. Pope,* A Survey of Persian Art, *vol. I, fig. 103)*

above it, stood either side of the large one. All was now of stone, even the roofing. The halls now stood in the smaller
Fig. 34 portion of a vast rectangular court, which was divided into two by a wall. Further *iwans* were added to the original two
Fig. 35 groups of the main temple, and a strange square building at-tached to the back. The smooth interior walls of this main tem-
Fig. 36 ple group were given attractive sculptured details: door – frames
Plates 23, 64, 66, were richly carved, and theatre masks added to internal pilasters.
68 The entire length of the front façade was united by a decorative system of half-columns and arches, and was probably crowned by a continuous attic. The profile of the arches was often rendered
Plate 68 as two Ionic *fasciae*. But the addition of the heads or upper portions of divine figures to some of the stone voussoirs of the arches and the frequent misuse of classical mouldings indicate a refusal to follow slavishly the dictates of Roman fashion. Close by in the western court stood separate *iwan* buildings.

Most of these were architecturally similar to the main group but connected with it only by alignment. The shrine of Shahru (Andrae's Building D), however, was more obviously a temple in the Graeco-Roman sense, for it boasted a porch of six columns, each of superimposed limestone drums. The western court was itself subdivided by a cross-wall. The over-all planning of this group of buildings is curiously unsatisfactory. Arched gateways, with mouldings of classical type and rich carving, led through to the larger eastern court. Here stood the so-called Hellenistic Temple (Andrae E), which would have been of

Fig. 37

Fig. 36 Doorway of the Sanctuary of Shamash, behind the great South Iwan, Hatra, second century AD (after W. Andrae, Hatra (II), 1912, fig. 254)

Fig. 34(D)

orthodox eastern Roman type had not the builders placed a pair of columns actually upon the front steps. The drill-work visible in the Corinthian column-capitals and entablature points to a date in the late second or earlier third century AD.

Further temples, mostly including courts and *iwans*, were raised in clusters around the central sanctuary. They too began as brick and ended as limestone, and their plans show connex-ions with temples of Babylonia and of contemporary Dura and Syria. They have yielded rich treasures of sculpture to their Iraqi excavators. Even in decay, when the city had been de-stroyed by the Sasanians, the gigantic *iwans* of the Hatrene temples retained an air of simple grandeur. The sight of them is enough to explain why the Arabs who beheld the echoing ruins of the deserted city wove stories of Hatra and its princes into their legends.

Fig. 35

The square building attached to the back of the *iwans* of the Sun temple of Hatra is one of a distinct group of Parthian reli-gious buildings. One such we have already encountered within the mausoleum of New Nisa. An example at Kuh-i Khwaja must have been a fire temple, for an overturned fire altar was found within it lying beside its brick base. The building dom-

Fig. 28(B)

inated the whole 'palace'. Built of sun-dried brick in the first century AD, it possessed a square central chamber surrounded by an enclosed corridor. The chamber roofing consisted of a peculiar 'squinch-vault', a direct forerunner of the later Sasanian dome on squinches that was used in fire temples and other im-portant buildings. The shrine at Hatra was dedicated to the Sun-god Shamash. Here too a square central chamber, roofed

Plate 25

with a barrel vault, was completely surrounded by a corridor, also vaulted. Two staircases were set into the walls, at least one of which reached the roof. The shrine was added on to the back of the already completed *iwans*. The rough-and-ready character of Hatrene architecture is well illustrated by the trouble that the builders encountered in driving a door through the back wall

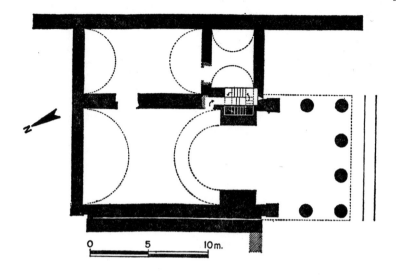

Fig. 37 Plan and front façade of the Temple of Shahru, Hatra, probably second century AD *(after W. Andrae,* Hatra (II), *1912, pl. VI)*

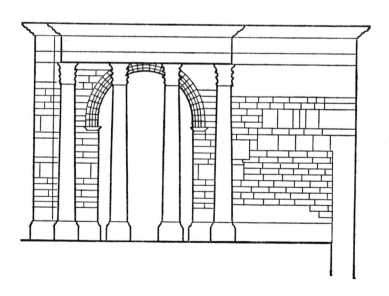

Fig. 36

of the south *iwan* to provide an entrance into this shrine. First, they drove the doorway through on the axis of the shrine. But then they realised that this was distressingly off-centre in the back wall of the *iwan*, where it was prominently visible. So they walled up this entrance, leaving the relieving arch over the door still set into the wall, and drove a second doorway through beside the first, but now on the axis of the south *iwan*. This was now naturally off-centre in the shrine, but this lack of symmetry was less noticeable in the narrow corridor of Shamash's sanctuary. Obviously, no one had fully considered the effect of the door's position in advance. Whether fire worship took place here is unknown. The square plan of these shrines, however, is distantly derived from those of Achaemenid fire temples and was later taken over and adapted by Sasanian builders for their fire sanctuaries.

Plate 25

The enclosing corridor and the square central chamber were both important Iranian features of a unique temple found at Taxila (Jandial), now in north-west Pakistan. But the temple, datable to the Scytho-Parthian period, also shows amazingly Greek features in its general layout and in the Ionic columns of its entrance. Perhaps the closest Parthian parallel is the Peripteros of Assur. The rear third of the *cella* (cult-room) was walled off from the front portion of the temple and could be entered only from the back part of the corridor, which was well lighted by numerous windows. Here an entrance flanked by engaged columns opened into a narrow passage and staircase which led to the now ruined upper part of the building, used perhaps for the worship of fire or for some local cult. The brickwork of the temple was covered with a fine stucco of crushed shells, a peculiarity of the region mentioned by Philostratus, whose life of Apollonius of Tyana badly needs such touches of realism.

Fig. 32(D)

The use of stucco, often gaily painted, as a covering to protect and brighten buildings, was a custom of long standing in the ancient world. In the Near East, ornament in relief, in the form

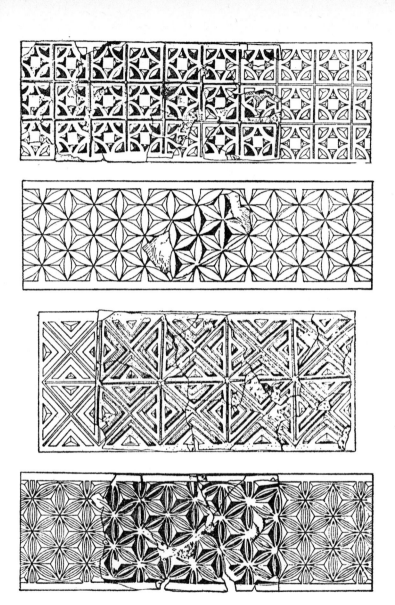

Fig. 38   Sections of stucco decoration from Assur, later Parthian period (after W. Andrae, Die Partherstadt Assur, *pl. 15)*

of animals, friezes and so on, was added where required in moulded bricks, which were coated with plaster or coloured and glazed. One brick might carry one unit of the design, or else the unit might run over several bricks together. In the Parthian period, this type of ornament became very rare. But in the first century AD there was a sudden flowering across the Parthian area of the creation in the stucco itself of decorative designs. These were applied to prominent parts of a building and picked out with brilliant colours. This decorative plaster appeared in courtyards, *iwans*, entrances and important rooms, and was used in particular on arches, mouldings, ceilings and columns. The plaster was made by heating gypsum and then mixing water with the resultant powder. Close examination of the stucco found at Seleucia on the Tigris showed that it had been worked when already in position, as the edges were sharp and clear-cut. Examples of this stucco discovered as far apart as Assur and Kuh-i Khwaja all belong to a common decorative repertoire. Hellenistic Greek motifs predominate. Acanthus leaves, the key-pattern, spiralling vines, egg-and-dart, and square coffers all occur frequently. These designs were also common all over the Roman east. But Oriental designs, such as rosettes and stepped battlements, are also found. The only important site where such decorative stucco does not occur is Nisa, where the local craftsmen applied architectural ornament in moulded terracotta. The stucco was so simple and quick to work that old decorative forms were easily maltreated and tended to emerge in strange new guises. The Ionic capital, for instance, suffered harshly indeed. It is impossible to say where this method of decoration originated, for it appears on both sides of Parthia at roughly the same time, as did the *iwan*. But it was very likely an Iranian invention, and one with an influential future. The Sasanians adopted and improved Parthian methods and ultimately the coloured architectural stucco was to be transmuted into the Persian tile.

Fig. 38

Plates 24, 27

Fig. 39

Fig. 39   Ionic entablature in brick and stucco of peristyle of the Parthian palace at Assur, first century AD *(after W. Andrae,* Die Partherstadt Assur, *fig. 34)*

In engineering and the techniques of building construction the Parthian architects were no match for their western neigh‑ bours, the Romans. This was due partly to local circumstances.

Materials available encouraged brick rather than stone architecture, but the components of Roman concrete were not plenti-
fully to hand. Nor were the possibilities even of brick architecture exploited as fully as they might have been. Nevertheless,
certain developments emerged during the Parthian period.
Fig. 40 Some curious methods of bricklaying were found at Assur.
Certain walls of fired brick were laid in courses which alternated
between the usual horizontal course and the vertical. Even
more interesting was the builders' method of making a column
out of bricks. These were arranged like the slices of a cake, and
the whole column was then covered with an icing of gypsum
plaster. This method of bricklaying was later adopted by the
Sasanians at Ctesiphon. Brick vaults, which had for centuries
been a feature of Babylonian architecture, albeit a minor one,
were now popular and sometimes constructed on a considerable
scale. The improvement of gypsum mortar, so that it dried
very quickly, made this possible. The palace of Assur contained
one of the more complex Parthian examples. A hall was
Fig. 40 roofed with a barrel vault which rested on a brick arcade. But
even here the vault is simple. It rises well above the arches, and
so sets no problems of intersection. The nearest the Oriental
builders of this period got to the exploration of such problems
was in the still simple squinch-vault of Kuh-i Khwaja. But
even these vaults were seemingly exceptional. The true inferior-
ity of Parthian engineering technique comes out in their stone
buildings. Of these, the temples of Hatra constitute by far the
most important examples. Walls are faced with well-cut limestone blocks on each side and contain a rubble core. The Sun
Plate 68 Temple shows examples of pseudo-isodomic masonry, wherein
thin blocks alternate with wide. Most of the halls of the temples
Plate 25 and the chambers of the tombs were roofed with stone vaults.
Again this roofing is of the simplest kind of barrel-vaulting – a
straight tunnel with no intersections. There are two principal
kinds of barrel-vault, the commoner type being constructed in

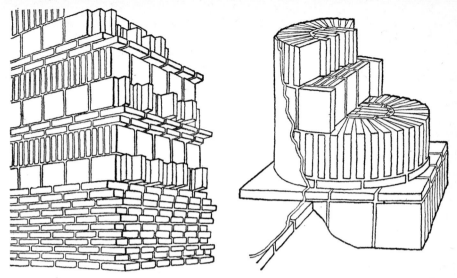

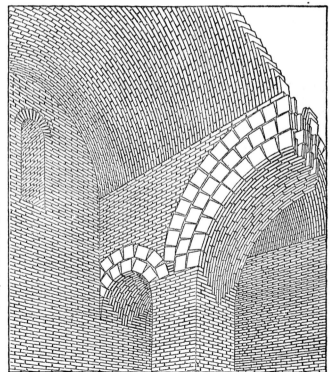

Fig. 40 Examples of brick-laying at Assur, showing the arrangement of fired bricks in walls and columns and in the vaulting of the Parthian palace, first century AD (after A. U. Pope, A Survey of Persian Art, vol. I, figs. 99–100)

Fig. 41

ordinary keystone masonry. Some of the smaller rooms of the
Sun Temple, however, were roofed by a series of stone arches
set close enough together to support flat stone beams laid across
the gaps between them, a Roman practice also. In either case,
the spandrels above were filled with rubble so as to create a flat
floor or rooftop above. The thrust of the biggest vaults was
taken by thick supporting walls and by smaller side-chambers
which acted partly as buttresses. No attempt was made to emu-
late the complex cross-vaults and domes of contemporary Roman architecture. We may discount Philostratus' description
of a sapphire-domed chamber in Vardanes' palace at Babylon
as mere fiction. Moreover, the fifty-foot span of the widest vault
at Hatra was less than half the broadest already achieved by the
Romans. But simplicity of construction is no bar to grandeur.

It must already be clear that the influences which went into
the making of Parthian architecture were not only many and
diverse, but sometimes even opposed in principle. The most
serious problems which the builders encountered lay in the absorption of Greek, and later Roman, practice, for the principles
of these architectures, as well as the materials used, were quite
different from those of native tradition. Yet by the first century
AD these problems had been mastered. The Parthians solved the
question of how to use Greek architectural forms, the column,
architrave and so on, by doing just as the Romans had already
done: they turned them into applied decoration. Columns grew
into engaged half-columns or pilasters, and architraves became decorative friezes. The use of brick and the development
of decorative stucco made this all the easier. Naturally, as soon
as the precise function of each Greek element was lost, so its
part in a new role as decoration could be varied at will. This
freedom resulted in the creation of new and exotic decorative
Plate 27 schemes. The coloured façades of the *iwans* at Assur exemplify
what was possible. The design of these façades seems to be
vaguely derived from the combination of a Roman (or Hellen-

Fig. 41   One method of constructing a stone roof used in the main sanctuary, Hatra, probably c. 100 AD. *(After A. U. Pope,* A Survey of Persian Art, *vol. I, fig. 102)*

istic) triumphal arch with a typical theatre backdrop. The num‑ erous half‑columns, arranged in groups either side of arched recesses, have lost the bases, *entasis* (diminution) and subtle capitals of their Greek forebears. With their extreme slenderness and unsymmetrical arrangement, they are closer to the fluted façades of Babylonian architecture than to western forms. They rely for their effect on quantity, and 'support' architraves the decoration of which is paramount, and the function of which has so dwindled in importance that the panels of the façade are not even related to the rooms behind. The dominant feature of the whole façade is the arch, the entry into the *iwan*. The Parthian builders have ruthlessly plundered Greek forms and ornament, and totally transmuted what they found. In their stone architecture, they were less adventurous. The sanctuaries of Khurha and Kangavar, if they belong to the early Parthian period, were built on Greek lines even if strict Greek rules were ignored. The columns of Hatra, both free and engaged, were built up of superimposed stone blocks in the classical Greek manner; moreover, the columns show diminution in the upper third, a reminiscence of Greek *entasis*. The shrine of Shahru boasted a six-columned portico, the Hellenistic Temple even a peristyle. The 'Corinthian' capitals of Hatra, the double *fasciae* around the *iwan* arches, the Greek mouldings (if often in an unclassical position) all testify to strong eastern Roman influences, which have not been so fully transmuted as in the brick and stucco architecture. But however much they borrowed, the Parthians remained masters, not slaves, of the ideas that they took, and produced some powerful innovations of their own. The *iwan* is without sure precedent in the ancient east. Construction improved with the spread of gypsum mortar, and enabled the Parthians to raise the vault from relatively unimportant architectural functions to be the crown of their *iwan* halls. In the squinch-vault of Kuh-i Khwaja a first step was taken towards the Sasanian dome, and in the manifold uses of decorative and painted stucco lay the seeds of the later glories of tiling. The Parthians created architectural usages which their successors adopted and refined, and which have not yet ceased to influence the architecture of the Iranian regions.

Fig. 37

Fig. 36

CHAPTER VIII

Art

DESPITE THE RAVAGES OF TIME, abetted by Sasanian and later dynasties, sufficient works of Parthian art remain for at least a tentative account of its development to be possible. Three main stages are discernible. The first was one of eclecticism, when inspiration was sought in older Oriental and contemporary Greek styles. By the end of the first century BC, this mixture of styles had coalesced into a fairly coherent 'Parthian' style. Finally, in the later second and early third centuries AD, Parthian art seemingly went rotten at the centre. Royal and official art declined steeply in quality, leaving the preservation of artistic standards to vassal kingdoms and to communities on the fringes of the Parthian cultural area.

The introduction of Hellenistic Greek art with its fluid figure postures, illusionism and pictorial space was bound to give the traditional arts of the Orient a severe shaking-up. Rows of profile figures in stiff postures, low relief carving, a lack of interest in the scientific depiction of space, a love of decorative detail and the unrealistic patterning of drapery, a rigidly frontal statuary – these characteristics had been ingrained into the styles of the Near East over millennia. The Parthian artists were the first Orientals who had to cope with and absorb the impact of Hellenistic art.

Until the later first century BC, there is little sign of such absorption. Instead, artists were strongly influenced either by older regional artistic traditions or by the new Hellenistic style. Many using this style were of course of Greek descent themselves. This variation between Oriental and Greek style is particularly noticeable in the earlier issues of the Arsacid coinage, which always tended to reflect stylistic changes in the major arts. The coins of Mithradates I (*c.* 171–138 BC) show at least

Plate 6a, aa

four different styles. The coins struck by him apparently in north-eastern Iran portray his head in profile; he is beardless, and wears the pointed Saca cap or *bashliq*. The subject here is Iranian, the style modified Greek, like that used for his coins minted in central Iran. A third style, inspired by the Greek issues of Bactria, was used for coins minted presumably in the territory Mithradates had seized from king Eucratides. Finally, when he entered Seleucia, he used Demetrius' die-cutters to

Plate 6b, bb

issue splendid silver coins, with a fine profile of his head in full Seleucid Greek style. Thus Mithradates' coins vary in style and subject according to region and tradition.

This variation of style is still more striking in the major arts of this period. An incompetent sub-Achaemenian style was employed in the reliefs of a fire temple erected at Persepolis in the early Seleucid period. On the door jambs are represented a local governor or prince and his wife in attitudes of worship. Pieces of a male statue of the Seleucid period, carved in a rather less disheartening version of the same style, were found at Susa. These Persian traditions lived on in Phoenicia and Anatolia,

Fig. 4

and underlie the large Parthian rock relief of Mithradates II at Behistun. The king faces four of his vassals, who are arranged in a profile row before him according to rank. The type of scene is familiar from Achaemenian art, but all refinement is gone. Instead, the figures are cut in very low relief, and internal detail is rendered by engraved lines. Subtlety of modelling has succumbed to linearity.

Some Achaemenian influence can still be seen in the fine reliefs and statues carved by order of King Antiochus I of Commagene (69–34 BC) to decorate his enormous temple-tomb or *hierothesion* at Nemrud Dagh, in southern Anatolia. Here, above his capital city Arsameia on the Nymphaeus, he himself was to be an object of worship after his death, and here too were practised the cults of the syncretized Graeco-Persian

Plate 29

deities of Commagene. The sanctuary he built was grandiose.

It was surrounded on three sides by terraces and dominated by a mound nearly five hundred feet high. On the east and west terraces stood a row of five colossal seated figures, many times life-size, which represented four deities and Antiochus himself. Into the terrace walls were sunk some ninety stone reliefs, arranged as a dado and depicting in most cases a pair of figures, one of whom is again usually Antiochus. He is shown meeting his gods with a friendly handshake. We also see his paternal ancestors, traced back to the Achaemenid monarch Darius, son of Hystaspes (Vishtaspa), and the lion, symbol of Antiochus' constellation. Figures and statues are labelled in Greek. The hierothesion of Antiochus' father, Mithradates Kallinikos, at Arsameia has produced a similar series of reliefs. The soft contours and low relief of these figures, together with the patterned folds of drapery and delicate ornamentation of reliefs and statues, are all derived from Achaemenian tradition. From the Greek world the artists have taken some divine figures, notably Zeus and Heracles, to represent their local deities. But the high pointed tiara worn by the colossal statue of Heracles, the Persian tiara and the tunic, cloak and leggings of the god Apollo on the reliefs, and the royal Armenian headdress and Iranian costume of the king himself, are all items from the contemporary Parthian world. Moreover, these are not the only novelties here. The meeting and handclasp between god and king, and the scene on two battered reliefs in which Antiochus hands the diadem to his son and successor, together announce the creation of a new theme for Iranian art: the investiture, a staple subject for Sasanian monuments.

But if there is novelty here, the sanctuary as a whole was conceived in a tradition more ancient still than that of the Achaemenids. The guardian lions, the colossal statues of the terraces, the dado-reliefs are all unmistakable survivals of the monumental building practices of the Hittites. All these traditions are here welded into one mighty creation: indeed, the unwary visi-

Plate 31

Plate 30

tor to the sanctuary might imagine that he had stumbled upon the last resting place rather of a Rameses of Egypt than of a minor kinglet of southern Anatolia.

In other areas, other traditions lived on. Five hundred years of squalor and political nonentity in what had once been Assyria were still not enough to erase from memory the style of Assyrian art. About 89/8 BC two tall gravestones were carved in the town of Assur. Although the bearded man depicted on each was shown wearing Parthian tunic and trousers, the sculptors still worked in basically the old tradition. The depth of relief is low, the stele has a curved top and the men are shown in profile, as before; ancient religious symbols of Assyria appear beside each head. Some Assyrian traits mixed with Greek characteristics can also be observed in a little head of greenish-black stone found somewhere in northern Mesopotamia. The beard, the hairstyle and the diadem recall some coin portraits of Mithradates I, and this head may represent that monarch.

It is hardly surprising that Greek art should be much in evidence during this early period. Nisa has produced objects of great interest, including many from the first couple of centuries of Parthian rule. The most remarkable discoveries were made in the wrecked 'treasure house' of Old Nisa. Scattered through the rooms of this house, lying where robbers had spurned them for more precious loot, were weapons, shield bosses, terracotta

Plate 32

Fig. 42   Top section of an ivory rhyton found at Nisa with a band of figured decoration. In the main field, a procession accompanies an animal; above, a row of heads. Ht about 2 in. (5 cm.). Probably second century BC. (After Union Soviétique, December 1954)

Fig. 43   Units of terracotta decoration from the mausoleum, Nisa, of the earlier Parthian period. (After A. U. Pope, A Survey of Persian Art, *vol. I, fig. 114)*

figures, painted and fluted glass, pottery, Hellenistic metal figurines of Athena, Eros and a Sphinx, and above all some finely
carved ivory objects. These included the foot of a throne, shaped
as a griffin's claw grasping leaves, and a whole group of magnificent rhytons or drinking horns. Not only were these rhytons
embellished with inset stones, coloured glass and gold, but
around the rims they bore figures illustrating scenes from Greek   *Fig. 42*
mythology and sometimes also rows of heads. The horns ended
in a carved figure, a winged Centaur, lion or goddess. At least
two artistic traditions are amalgamated here. The shape of the
horns is derived from that of Achaemenian rhytons. The mythological scenes are Greek, and rendered in a Greek way. But the
decorative rows of heads are an Iranian feature of Parthian art,
seen also, for instance, around the *iwan* arches of the Hatra temples. Other discoveries echo this variation in style. Greek art
offers two Hellenistic marble statuettes of women or goddesses;   *Fig. 3*
a head of Heracles, however, probably in fact represents Verethragna, by assimilation. Fragments of clay statues of indeter-   Plate 3
minate style found in the 'palace' perhaps belonged to figures of
royal ancestors. Numbers of architectural fragments in terra-   *Fig. 43*
cotta show a mixture of Greek and oriental forms and themes.
The old Assyrian stepped merlon appears again. Upturned
arrows, the crescent, a club and other items which appear

on terracotta plaques are perhaps to be interpreted as Iranian divine symbols.

The closeness of the Parthian site of Nisa to the strongly Hellenised kingdom of Bactria raises the important question whether influence from the Graeco-Bactrian style is present here. The fine coins of Bactria, the portrait head of Euthydemus and the recent discoveries at the site of Aï Khanum in Afghanistan all testify to the quality of Bactrian art. Of these, Aï Khanum (occupied *c.* 300 to 100 BC) is for us the most important. The site has yielded fragments of statues which are Greek in style, but made of clay, and architectural fragments reminiscent of some at Parthian Nisa. These are the first signs of an indisputable artistic connexion.

About the beginning of our era, we see the rapid emergence from this medley of a more or less coherent and unified 'Parthian' style in the arts of the Empire. This style seems to have been evolved in the Mesopotamian region. Like all artistic styles it is subject to a certain amount of regional variation, but there is an underlying unity previously absent. Its emergence is heralded by changes that had been taking place in the designs of Parthian coins during the first century BC. The purely Greek coins disappeared for ever, and the coins of 'Oriental' style were rendered in an increasingly uniform and linear manner. Around the opening of our era, coins tend to show the king's head as a series of raised lines only. His features, along with his hair and diadem, have all been subordinated to an Oriental love of pattern. These linear patterns and the abandonment of realistic modelling are prominent features of the emergent 'Parthian' style. Motifs from a wide range of sources, Oriental and Greek, are absorbed. The figures of Greek deities continue to be used to represent their Oriental counterparts.

By an amusing trick of fate, the earliest known examples of truly 'Parthian' art were found on a site not strictly Parthian at all. They were discovered at Palmyra, politically in Roman

Plate 6

Fig. 44   Relief of soft limestone, found beneath the court of the Temple of Bel, Palmyra, with a man and two women worshippers in profile beside a man or priest who throws incense on to an altar. Probably late first century BC. *Ht about 2 ft (60 cm.). (After M. More- bart,* Berytus, *1956–7, p. 53 f.)*

Syria but on the western fringes of the Parthian cultural area. When our era began, Palmyra was an up-and-coming town growing from the profits of the caravan trade beside an import- ant oasis in the Syrian desert. The earliest remnants of Palmyr- ene art yet discovered were found deliberately buried in a trench, dug before AD 32 in the precinct of the still awe-inspiring Tem- ple of Bel. These woefully unimpressive pieces of sculpture are the sections and fragments of small reliefs, which had clearly once decorated the Bel temple's undoubtedly squalid predeces- sor and were no longer needed. Yet they are of immense value for the history of Parthian art. A few of them once showed a row of figures in profile, a standard subject for the art of western Asia that was now millennia old. But among these files of fig- ures, two stand out. One shows a man at an altar; unlike the

Fig. 44

rest of the figures in the scene, who are seen in profile, he is turned so that he almost faces to the front. The second shows a similar scene, but the officiant's position is completely frontal. These reliefs mark the arrival of a new and revolutionary principle in Near Eastern art: frontality. Attemps to connect its appearance with earlier isolated manifestations of frontality in Oriental and Greek styles have failed. Within a few decades, this method of arranging the figures of a scene had become almost universal in Parthian art. The participants in a scene or action are no longer related to one another logically: they all turn their gaze, and frequently their entire bodies also, towards the spectator. When one considers that for more than three thousand years Oriental practice had involved the almost exclusive use of the profile view for figures in relief and painting, with just a few standard exceptions, the magnitude of this change in the traditional arts of the east becomes apparent.

Plates 34–36, 38–39

The principles of this new Parthian style are all put into practice in certain religious scenes which were carved to decorate the temple of Bel at Palmyra, dedicated on 6 April, AD 32. The colonnaded portico or peristyle around the temple was linked to the *cella* by great limestone beams which once supported a peristyle roof. Each of the two sides of every beam bears a religious scene, cut in low relief and originally picked out with colouring. No general scheme can be detected in the allotment of religious scenes to these beams: they seem to have been contributed haphazardly by individual donors. In an example such as the 'Battle of the Gods against the Snake-legged Giant' the gods are attacking the giant vigorously on foot and horseback, in a scene from some forgotten Oriental myth. There is no attempt to render the space in which this is happening. The spectator would have 'read' the iconography of the scene as a battle, and identified the deities by their clothing and emblems in the same way as his ancestors had done for many centuries. But every deity who participates in the scene, even when leap-

Plates 35, 36

Fig. 45

ing at the giant on horseback, faces the spectator. The effect of this new convention is to draw us, the spectators, into the scene. Our relationship with the divinities represented has become personal.

The speed with which frontality overthrew the ancient profile view was amazing. Frontality invaded Palmyra around the end of the first century BC. By AD 32, the date of the Bel beam reliefs, profile figures have become obsolete at Palmyra, or are at most to be tucked into the corners of a scene to represent subordinate persons. After the period of these reliefs, frontality reigns supreme in Palmyrene art. Religious reliefs dated AD 31/32 and 54 from Dura Europos also show the new convention; and thereafter it spreads fairly rapidly all over the regions of Mesopotamia, Babylonia and western Iran. The now badly weathered rock carving at Behistun of AD 50, in which we see king Gotarzes II on horseback spearing an enemy, is still done

in the old profile convention. Yet this *scene*, the combat between two horsemen, was to have a long life in later Parthian
and Sasanian art. Another royal relief of roughly the same
period, placed on a rock face at Hungi Azdar in western Iran,
belongs to the transitional phase. A horseman in profile approaches four frontal figures, who are perhaps paying homage
to him. Thereafter, in western Parthia, frontality dictates composition: a funerary stele at Assur, a religious scene at Behistun,
and a number of rock reliefs such as those of Shimbar and
Tangi Sarvak, all display it. Before the end of the first century
AD, frontality had spread beyond these regions and even to
eastern Iran, as we shall see. Its arrival poses interesting questions, not the least of which is why frontality was ever adopted.

Fig. 21

Plate 74

At its inception, frontality seems to have been a device to
mark out a prominent deity, figure or figures of a religious
scene, so as to bring them as it were into a personal relationship
with the spectator. Characters, normally those of lesser importance, might still be shown in profile, but they soon conformed as well. Thus the spectators of these reliefs were brought
into closer contact with the deities they worshipped, and with
the scenes in which these figures took part. A clue to the reason
why frontality appeared at this time in west Parthian art has been
sought in the contemporary political and theological conditions
of the western Parthian regions. In the eyes of the Semitic inhabitants of Mesopotamia, their local divinities had recently
scored a significant victory. The gods of the Seleucids had failed
to protect their worshippers, the Seleucid government had
fallen, and the Semitic *baals* had triumphed. An upsurge of
national feeling and selfconfidence among the once subject
populations followed. Their language, Aramaic, became a
local official language in a number of cities of the area, Palmyra,
Dura, Assur and Hatra included, and remained so even when
foreign domination, Parthian or Roman, was again established.
This national feeling, when combined with recently developed

Fig. 11

religious and philosophical conceptions of the importance of the individual, produced the desire among the Semitic populations for closer personal contact with their deities through their images. Frontality, it is suggested, was the means by which they achieved this. Once introduced, the convention entered all spheres of art across – and ultimately beyond – the Empire.

The rest of the religious scenes on the peristyle beams of the temple of Bel at Palmyra already illustrate many of the principal themes of Parthian religious art: the gods and goddesses in hieratic, frontal rows; the offering of incense on a small burner set beside the worshipper; and the mythological picture. Like their earlier Oriental predecessors, the Parthian artists had no desire to create pictorial space, nor indeed to give their figures much solidity. An intention to invent an original composition was far from their minds. Instead, we find above all the repetition of traditional formulae. Divinities are marked by attributes; their gestures, poses and costumes are standardised; whole scenes are repeated again and again. The scenes are meant to be 'read' by the spectator with the traditional aids rather than realism to help him. Spiritual meaning, not mere illusion, is the artists' aim.

Some of the Bel temple religious scenes are fairly complicated. In the 'Arab Religious Procession', for instance, the designer had to include numbers of spectators of the main event, the passage of the palanquin or *qobba* borne on camel-back. These spectators are not arranged along one ground line, or in receding planes: on the left of the scene, one group is simply raised up above another, in a composition which has close affinities with much older Oriental work such as Assyrian relief. The group of shrouded women on the right, however, whose all-enclosing garments have been transformed into a play of line and pattern, form one of the most remarkable – and original – creations of Parthian art. Another relief shows us the handshake of the

Plate 34

Plate 36

moon-god Aglibol and his agrarian colleague Malakbel, whose powers are demonstrated by the twin altars heaped with products of the earth beside them. Incidentally, Aglibol's masculinity was ruthlessly ignored by Greek workmen who were hired, most exceptionally, to carve a stone ceiling within the temple of Bel; for to the Greeks the Moon-deity, Selene, was female. They therefore represented the Moon as female within the temple, indifferent to Aglibol's masculinity on the reliefs of the peristyle immediately outside. This is doctrinal gibberish.

Hundreds of religious reliefs, most of them dedications rather than cult-reliefs, have been found in and around Palmyra. They are mostly small, and the majority show one or more deities, to whom incense is frequently being offered on a burner. The divinities are usually named, and requested to look kindly on the dedicant, in Aramaic inscriptions. They often wear the working and riding clothes of the ordinary Palmyrene, and ride the same mounts, the horse and camel. Most of these deities, even goddesses, are armed for the better protection of their worshippers. At other times a deity may be represented by a symbolic figure or emblem, such as the outstretched hand, the lion or the thunderbolt. The figures and attributes of the divinities generally are drawn from a variety of sources, Oriental, Greek and occasionally Roman. Thus the originally Canaanite god Shadrafa wears Hellenistic armour but is marked out by the old Mesopotamian symbols of the snake and the scorpion. Unfortunately, the artists too often economised drastically in the number of figure-types that they used. When their usual emblems are absent, the frequently identical figures are certainly indistinguishable to us and were so, one would have thought, to the Palmyrenes as well.

The best-known examples of Palmyrene art to have survived are the stone relief busts which were originally intended to house the *nefesh* or spirits of the Palmyrene dead – and not to hang on museum walls. Their form is inspired by that of

Plates 34, 38
Plate 38

Plate 34

Roman tombstones. Each of these slabs was used within the tomb to close up the end of the coffin compartment in which the mummified body of the person 'represented' was laid. They now give us a vivid picture of the outward appearance of the wealthier Palmyrenes – merchants, priests, immigrants, fashion‚ able women, children and eunuchs, in their Parthian and Greek clothes. These are not portraits in our sense, in spite of their sometimes astonishingly life‚like appearance. The discov‚ eries of two totally different busts of the same woman and two identical busts of different women are enough to prove this. Instead, identities are established by inscriptions, usually in Aramaic and less often in Greek, placed beside their heads. A vast amount of information may be drawn from these reliefs, and new motifs such as the frontal cross‚legged sitting posture adopted for the representation of Sasanian royal figures are al‚ ready apparent. The richest of the Palmyrenes had themselves depicted on much larger reliefs at a religious ceremony, the 'funerary banquet', at which they recline on an ornamented couch and are attended by their family. These reliefs, like much ancient sculpture, were once picked out with colour. The original appearance of a Palmyrene tomb interior has been impressively reconstructed in the Damascus Museum.

Every colonnaded street of Palmyra, every public place and every great religious sanctuary graced with columns was once lined with countless bronze statues, which were set up to honour merchants, leaders and benefactors of the city. Each statue stood high on a bracket which projected outwards half‚ way up every column, and sometimes from walls as well: un‚ doubtedly once a magnificent sight in the Syrian sunshine. Even the bare columns impress the visitor today. A strange re‚ creation of this lost sight greeted the famous traveller Lady Hester Stanhope on her entry into Palmyra in the last century. As she rode down the main colonnade, on every column bracket stood a lovely Arab girl, picked for her beauty to occupy this

Plate 37

Plates 40–46

Plate 39

Plate 46

Plate 37

position and waving in welcome to the visitor. A few lime-stone statues dimly recall this ancient grandeur: those, for instance, of some dignitaries, whose mediocrity is reflected in their memorials. In quite another class, however, are the fine, if

Plate 33

headless, funerary statues of two priests, found in the tomb tower known locally as Qasr el-abiad, the White Castle. Carved of the best limestone and finished with the greatest care, these pieces demonstrate the sophistication achieved by the Palmyrene sculptors by about AD 100. The priests wear the customary Parthian tunic and trousers, with the addition of cloak, belt and extra leggings. The two statues are so alike that the same sculptor probably carved both of them. The garments are edged with decoration, in which the careful carving testifies to the sculptor's enjoyment in doing it. Vine scrolls, beaded edging and Greek 'wave crest' make up his repertoire, and the sparing use of this decoration creates paradoxically an impression of richness. The figures stand facing squarely to the front. The dignity and repose created by this posture are lightened by pleasing proportions and by the delicate play which the sculptor has made with the patterns of drapery folds, subtly varied to conceal the simple symmetry which is the basis of the scheme.

Plate 51

A similar effect is created by the tall bronze statue of a local chieftain found at Shami in the Bakhtiari mountains, not very far from Susa. It was unearthed in the ruins of the small shrine in which the local cults of Greek divinities and of deified royal

Plate 1

persons were probably practised. The battered bronze heads of a Seleucid monarch and his wife, perhaps Antiochus IV Epiphanes and his queen, were also discovered among the debris of the sanctuary, together with the marble head of a Greek goddess. The chieftain stands in Parthian dress, daggers at his side and a metal torque round his neck. The diadem that he wears is imitated from that of the Parthian King of kings, and is of a type seen on coins of around 50 BC and after. The statue was therefore probably made between then and about AD 100. The hair is attractively arranged in a style that falls to the shoulders; a thick, wide moustache is contrasted with the engraved lines that indicate the hair of his beard and chest. The head is strictly too small for the body: it was made separately, and perhaps head and body were cast in different places. The effect of this disproportion is to increase his apparent height; his stance, and the basic symmetry of the composition, give him an air of solid/ity and authority. No one can doubt that he is in the presence of a ruler. Plate 47

A marble head, also found at Shami, obviously represents another such local chieftain. His hair and diadem are similar to those of his bronze counterpart, but some important differences in style are detectable. The modelling of his face, the furrowed brow and a certain softness of execution are in complete con/trast with the smoother planes and crisper workmanship of the bronze head. This may be the product of an artist trained in a workshop with Greek traditions, but employed to realise a Parthian subject. Also perhaps from the western part of the Iranian plateau comes the statuette of a chieftain in Parthian dress and hair/style, and the little bronze bust of a ruler that once probably formed the top of a sceptre: its resemblance to the coin portraits of Orodes III (*c.* AD 4–7) is no compliment to that ruler. Plate 48

Plate 49

The Arab princes of Hatra, however, are the vassals of the Parthians who have left behind them the most splendid memo/rials of their existence. In the second century AD the rulers and aristocrats of Hatra set up their marble effigies in the temples of the city which clustered around the huge central sanctuary of the Sun. So suddenly and so completely was the city destroyed around AD 240 that these statues simply remained standing on their pedestals or lay where they fell, buried under debris and totally forgotten. Now they have been recovered. King Uthal and king Sanatruq, whose name lived on in Arab legend, and the nobles and princesses of their courts, stand before us again Plate 50
Plate 65
Plates 52, 53, 55

in effigy. Rigidly frontal, completely immobile, they overwhelm the spectator by their piercing, even contemptuous glance. Their power and riches are visible in every patterned fold of their luxurious drapery, in the care of their elaborate coiffures, and in every pearl and jewel with which their costumes are adorned. But these statues are not mere copies of the living: their very un-lifelikeness emphasises the spiritual quality of this art. We see rather a powerful embodiment of the monarchic spirit; rulers of magnitude and their entourage, who stand face to face with the deity whom they worship by the gesture of the upraised hand.

The gods and goddesses of Hatra, too, are now known to us. In the temple of Ashur-Bel, the cult statue of the deity was discovered. The head, now gone, must once have had an almost Assyrian aspect. The costume and the figure of Tyche at his feet are derived from Greek art, but the style is Parthian. A brightly painted relief depicts for us a fierce, bearded deity in Parthian dress who holds a three-headed dog on a chain. This god must be Hades, lord of the dead, or rather a Semitic or Iranian equivalent, Nergal or Ahriman, for the dog is clearly Cerberus from the Greek underworld. The seated goddess, the snakes, scorpions and double-axe are drawn from Syrian and Mesopotamian religion. Composition is wanting: the figures and objects simply fill up the field, and symbolic value outweighs artistic considerations. Further sculptures show us the Eagle and standard of Hatra, a Medusa figure, a Moon-goddess and rows of frontal deities. The Greek figure of Athena represents the Arab goddess Allat, and a local god is depicted in the guise of several statues of Heracles, on which the sculptors seem to have vented all their Semitic repugnance for the nude. Little alabaster figurines constituted a cheaper type of religious dedication for the pious. The Sun and Moon gods are represented, as are further local gods of Greek form, such as Hermes with winged cap and sandals. Yet there can have been few at Hatra who knew who 'Hermes' was.

Plate 54

Fig. 46

Plates 56–64

Plate 60

Plate 59

Plate 63a, b

Fig. 46   Religious relief in limestone from Hatra. The central god holds an axe and the lead of the triple dog on the right; to his right, the Standard of Hatra, and to his left a goddess, perhaps Atargatis. In the field, symbolic snakes and scorpions. Probably second century AD

159

The heads, busts and figures of many of these deities are again reproduced on the façades and lintels of the temples. They are to be seen around the outer arched openings of the *iwans* in the enclosure of the Sun temple. Within, on the pilasters, remark able heads reminiscent of Greek and Roman theatre masks are carved. Almost certainly these had some ritual significance. Lintels carry further figures: the bust of Shamash, or a god reclining among acolytes. Finally, as guardian of the Sun Temple, a diminutive winged griffin is sculpted beneath one impost block of the northern *iwan* entrance. This is a distant descendant of the colossal winged and human headed bulls and lions that once protected the palaces of Assyria and Persepolis: a remote and unworthy progeny of so great a breed.

Plate 66

Plate 68

Plate 64

The hieratic dignity of Parthian sculpture permeates the wall paintings of Dura Europos. Here remarkable frescoes survived, particularly in buildings hastily filled up with earth to improve the defences of the city at the time of its final siege in the mid third century AD. During the period of Parthian domination between 113 BC and AD 164 the art of Dura became to a considerable extent Parthian in style, in spite of the Macedonian Greek foundation of the city. Statues and reliefs stood in the sanctuaries, and wall paintings adorned the chapels and houses of the inhabitants. The Parthian statuary of Dura is mostly naïve by comparison with the art of its neighbours Palmyra and Hatra. It shows the same characteristics, and frontality too was adopted by AD 31/2, as the bas relief of Zeus Kyrios shows and the stele of Aphlad of AD 54 confirms. A curious relief of rushing animals seems to be connected with the art of the nomad regions north of Iran. But the prime contribution of Dura to our knowledge of Parthian art lies in the sphere of painting. The brightly decorated chapels of the temples, with their rows of painted figures and cult niches, bore a striking resemblance to Orthodox Christian churches. The best preserved of these temples, that usually called the Temple of the Pal-

Plate 67

Fig. 22

myrene Gods and probably dedicated to Bel, illustrates clearly
the main characteristics of Durene religious painting. On the
back wall of the main hall of the temple, the god himself was
shown frontally, colossal in size and standing above a chariot.
On the side walls, in superimposed rows, were painted groups
of worshippers, all facing to the front: they mostly throw incense
into the flames of a small burner or *thymiaterion* set beside
them, or raise the right hand in a gesture of reverence. From
inscriptions and differences in style, it has been deduced that
this portion of the decoration was added section by section be/
tween AD 50 and 100. In a striking group we see the act of wor/
ship performed by the family of Conon, with priests in attend/   Plate 70
ance. The repetition of the figures' poses, the intense and
brooding gaze of the worshippers, the elimination of inessentials
all contribute to the spiritual and hieratic effect. Further scenes
were painted in a side/chapel and an outer cult/room was added
later to the original hall. For the outer *cella*, the pious donated
scenes, again arranged in rows, of more worshippers and gods
and of a sacrifice to a reclining goddess. In the mid second cen/
tury the eunuch Otes added the side/chapel in which he and
others were pictured making offerings to five Palmyrene deities.
Then, when Dura had fallen into Roman hands, a Roman
tribune named Terentius had a large painting added to this
ensemble, in which he himself and a priest worship three Pal/
myrene military gods and the Spirits *(Tychae)* of the cities of
Palmyra and Dura. Just as we saw at Palmyra, no over/all plan
was worked out for these scenes, which were added more or
less haphazardly as and when devotees chose to pay for them.

Sections and fragments of similar scenes and compositions
in other temples of Dura were likewise typical of those tradi/
tional in the western Parthian regions. This tradition was strong
enough to transform into the Parthian style paintings and reliefs
ordered by the Roman soldiers billeted in Dura from AD 164 on/
wards. Thus the tribune Terentius' act of worship is expressed

Plate 69

through the traditional formulae, and the Parthian style is again used for the paintings and reliefs of Mithras in the temple dedicated to him by the Romans. Much of this tradition survived in the quite extraordinary paintings of the Jewish Synagogue of Dura, decorated between about AD 245 and 255: haphazard donation of the individual illustrations of Old Testament themes, arrangement of the wall-space in registers, two-dimensional scenes and frontality all reappear. But these were executed a quarter of a century after the fall of the Arsacids, and so it is not for us to speak of them here.

Fig. 28

Plate 71

The other outstanding group of paintings of the Parthian period and area takes us to the opposite side of Iran, and to the 'palace' of Kuh-i Khwaja, Seistan. Insects are no respecters of art, and the paintings suffered severely from their ravages. These decorated the walls of the Long Gallery of the 'palace' in its earlier phase, which is usually dated to the first century AD. Along the window-wall, gods stood one partly behind another, motionless and almost completely turned to the front. On the back wall, up against the hillside, a king and queen appeared. The monarch puts his arm around his wife, and the couple were shown in three-quarters view. Around the windows of the gallery were the figures of spectators, rendered in full profile. These scenes signal the advent of frontality in this area. The divine figures were frontal, the mortal progressively further in profile according to rank. But even more remarkable than this is the undeniable fact that the paintings had an astonishingly Greek aspect, both in style and the motifs used, to such an extent that they can hardly be included in what we have just described as 'Parthian' art. The gods' garments were Greek. One of them wore a winged helmet, like the Greek Hermes, although here the helmet had three wings and was an emblem of Verethragna, and another held the trident of Poseidon, here the symbol of the Indian Shiva. The overlapping of the divine figures and the three-quarters view of the royal persons were alike devices borrowed from Hellenistic Greek art, as was much of the repertoire of figures and patterns used to decorate the ceiling, which included Eros on horseback and other Greek motifs. The Greek aspects of these paintings outweighed those, such as the rosettes and profile spectators, which seem to have been more traditionally Oriental and to have survived from Achaemenid art. The fact that Greek art was so strongly in evidence east of the Parthian realm when Parthian art further west had assimilated it far more fully has set art historians a puzzle which has not been solved yet. The problem of these paintings raises the whole question of the styles of art which grew up in the areas east of the Parthian Empire. These styles are related, sometimes closely, to Parthian art, but again surprisingly Greek (or Roman?) elements are present. Are these Mediterranean influences due to the effects of a now lost Greek art of Bactria which survived the collapse of the Graeco-Bactrian kingdom? Are they owed to Graeco-Roman influences permeating northwards from Roman trade with India, or to some as yet unknown influence from Parthia itself – or to a combination of all three?

Parthian subjects were never averse to Greek or Roman art. Many objects inspired by Hellenistic Greek art have turned up in early Parthian levels. From the first century BC, when Parthian art developed, it was normal for cities where this art was practised sometimes to import Graeco-Roman statues, objects and even artists. Thus at Palmyra a group of attractive marble statues imported about AD 200 has been found. Dura has yielded similar sculpture and polished marble statues were discovered at Hatra. To the Parthian period is commonly assigned also the vaguely Hellenised 'Lion of Hamadan', although this monstrous sculpture is now so weathered that only the boldest would dare to comment on its style. Perhaps Graeco-Roman bronze work was imported too, for the municipal tolls of Palmyra included a tax on imported bronze statues, two of

which made up a camel-load. We must not forget that many
of these cities contained considerable Greek populations. At
Plate 20   Seleucia on the Tigris, terracotta figurines were made in the
Greek style throughout most of the Parthian period, side by
side with others of Oriental aspect. Greek figures and deities
continued to appear alongside Oriental designs on seals
throughout Parthia, although the engraving tended to become
shallow. At Susa the delightful marble head of a woman was
unearthed, signed by a Greek artist. The subject, who wears a
Plate 72   tiara seemingly of royal Achaemenid derivation, has been tentatively identified as Musa, mother and wife of Phraataces (see
pp. 46 ff.). Apollonius of Tyana saw magnificent tapestries of
Greek style and subject hanging in king Vardanes' palace at
Babylon. But royal tastes do not seem to have been wholly in
accord with current trends in art. Although the king's coinage
was usually up-to-date, the rock relief of Gotarzes II, executed
in AD 50, was rendered in full profile, a device by that time already widely obsolescent.

No account of Parthian art can conceal the uneven concen-
tration of discoveries, nor the vast gap in our knowledge of the
art of Iran proper during this period. The Parthian style arose
first in the cities of the western fringe of the Empire, and then
spread eastwards until it dominated an area which extended
from the region of Palmyra in the west at least as far east as
central Iran. In the east of Iran, in Gandhara and in north-west
India, a number of related styles appeared, which we have not
had space to discuss. But it should at least be clear that Parthian
art represents one more phase in the over-all development of
western Asian styles, and the first to feel fully the powerful impact of Greek art. Its roots lay in the more ancient Orient. From
here it drew its linearity, hieratic quality and obsession with
detailed ornamentation. Staple Oriental subjects, war, divinities, sacrifice, hunting and banqueting, predominate. The revolutionary discoveries of the Greek artists affected their Par-

thian counterparts remarkably little: the Parthians picked out what they wanted from Greek art, and left the rest. Consequent, ly, although we find that the Parthian artists have borrowed many figures and motifs from Greek art, they have drawn few lessons from Greek knowledge of anatomy and modelling, and none at all from the Greek attempt to conquer pictorial space and the problems of perspective. Nor is there much sign of the influence of nomad art: Parthian art began in the cities. To the future, Parthian art contributed frontality (soon to permeate Roman art) together with some new motifs and scenes, includ, ing the offering of incense, the investiture, the combat on horse, back and the frontal cross,legged sitting posture. In treating their chosen subjects, the Parthian artists plainly thought as Orientals. Traditional symbols for figures, objects and actions replaced the Greek ideal of recreating nature in an aesthetically satisfying form. A mere couple of centuries of Greek domina, tion could not alter the Oriental artists' habits of mind which had been built up over more than three millennia.

CHAPTER IX

The Fall of the Arsacids

BY THE EARLY SECOND CENTURY AD, dynastic struggles had become a commonplace of Parthian politics. Osroes had been in the competition for the Parthian throne for decades by the time his last coin issues appeared in AD 128. Thereafter he dropped out, leaving the field to Vologases III (traditionally II) and to a usurper in Iran named Mithradates (IV), the latter known only from his coins. The defence of Parthia against a renewed menace seems to have fallen mainly to Vologases. About AD 135–6, the nomad horde of the Alani, incited by the petty monarch Pharasmanes of Iberia, again poured into the Empire from the north. They overran Media Atropatene, Armenia and even Cappadocia. Vologases sent twenty thousand foot-soldiers north from Ctesiphon but failed to stop them. Thereupon, we learn, either he bribed them to retire or they withdrew on hearing that their own homeland was threatened by other tribes.

Vologases may have had further trouble on the eastern frontier. By the first century AD the Saca dynasty of eastern Iran had given way to a new line of Indo-Parthian rulers, among whom the powerful Gondophares was ruling about AD 20–40. Indo-Parthian coins have been found from Merv to the Punjab. Soon after Gondophares' death, however, Afghanistan and the Punjab fell into the hands of the Yueh-chih dynasty of the Kushans, who created from them a sizeable kingdom. As the riches of India proved more attractive to the Kushans than conquest in Iran, both they and the Parthians seem to have been content to establish a common frontier which was roughly equivalent to that between Iran and Afghanistan today. The Romans opened contact with the Kushans, both as a political counter to Parthia and because they controlled alternative trade routes to China that ran north from the ports of India. The Kushans reached a peak of prosperity under their able but war- like king Kanishka. Oriental tradition records a war against the Parthians in his time. Kanishka may have been for at least part of his reign a contemporary of Vologases III. The precise period when Kanishka ruled, however, cannot be settled until it is established by what era the Kushan monuments are dated, and so the war cannot as yet be placed into its historical context.

In AD 147/8 appear the first coins of Vologases' successor, Vologases IV (III). He was to enjoy a reign which lasted more than forty years. Threatening moves which he made in the direction of Armenia were stopped for the time being by a strong letter from the Roman emperor and the movement of extra Roman troops to Syria. But there was little danger to the Parthians from the Romans for the moment; imperial policy did not favour intervention in Parthia, in spite of the arrival of embassies from the independent provinces of Hyrcania and Bactria. In AD 162, however, Vologases pressed Roman inac- tivity too far and invaded Armenia. His general Osroes trapped a Roman force and almost annihilated it; an Arsacid prince was placed on the throne of Armenia. Then the Parthian forces turned south and invaded Syria. The situation demanded ur- gent Roman action. The Parthians were known to have many friends in the province. Lucius Verus, co-emperor of Marcus Aurelius, was sent to drive out the invaders. He found the Syr- ian legions in as sorry a shape through decades of inertia as Corbulo had a century before. Verus himself took virtually no part in the ensuing campaign, preferring to leave the work to his officers. The army was drilled and exercised, and in 163 the Romans invaded Armenia, deposed the Parthian nominee and appointed one Sohaemus king. They then went further. In 164, by dint of a three-pronged attack on Mesopotamia and a bloody battle near Dura Europos, the Romans defeated the Parthian forces and advanced on Babylonia. Seleucia opened its gates, but shortly afterwards some agreement was broken and about December 165 the Romans ravaged the great city. Ctesiphon was also taken and Vologases' palace destroyed. But even at the moment of success, a totally unforeseen disaster struck the Romans. As the legionaries were looting Seleucia, plague swept through the army. Its attack was so fierce that much of the booty had to be left behind. Soldiers were dying continually on the march home; and the remainder carried the disease to the other ends of the Roman world. The fact that even Chinese records mention the plague indicates its force, and much of the Parthian Empire must also have been ravaged by it. Nevertheless, the Parthians probably retook most of their lost territory soon afterwards, for next year Verus' officers again invaded Mesopotamia, and Roman forces must have penetrated far enough east for Verus to call himself 'Medicus', victor in Media, on an issue of coins. But the Romans held few of their gains. By AD 170, the *status quo* had returned, except that Roman territories and influence spread further into northern Mesopotamia than before; Dura Europos was henceforth Roman. Vologases IV again threatened war to recover his losses about AD 175, but took no action.

Vologases V (IV) seemingly began to strike coins before his predecessor's death around AD 192, and used the troubles of the Romans in 193 to stir up rebellion in the now Roman kingdoms of Osroene and Adiabene. In 195 the emperor Septimius Severus recovered these districts, but was recalled to Europe for 196. Vologases swept through Mesopotamia and perhaps even Armenia, but his success was almost reversed by a revolt of 'Medes and Persians' which needed hard fighting in eastern Iran to suppress. This done, Vologases restored his control over Adiabene, pillaging several cities of the kingdom and drowning its obstinately pro-Roman monarch Narses in the Greater Zab. Next year Septimius Severus prepared to attack Parthia, raising new legions and constructing boats. In spring 198 he

advanced into Mesopotamia. The Parthians withdrew before him; and by autumn he had sacked the recalcitrant capital, Ctesiphon, and occupied the abandoned cities of Babylon and Seleucia. As food began to run short, however, the Romans soon had to begin a withdrawal up the Tigris. Like Trajan before him, Severus made an unsuccessful attack on Hatra as he passed. Next year he returned to Hatra with more provisions and better siege-engines. But his success was hardly any greater. The Hatrene cavalry attacked his foraging parties; and the defenders destroyed almost all his engines and discomfited numbers of his soldiers by hurling down jars of insects and 'Hatrene fire', a burning bituminous naphtha, upon the attackers. Hatrene engines fired two missiles simultaneously with great force and these even endangered the emperor's life. When the soldiers at last breached the walls and the city lay helpless before them, Severus gave the signal for retreat. The treasures of the sanctuary of the Sun were allegedly great: the prizes of assault went to the soldiers, but those of surrender, for which Severus hoped, to the commander. The angry soldiers retreated, and in one night the men of Hatra repaired the breach. There was no sign

Fig. 47

of surrender. Severus ordered a renewed assault, but the European soldiers, baulked of their loot, refused to move. The wretched Syrian troops, when ordered to attack, were slaughtered like sheep. Severus had to withdraw. The Romans had made no territorial gains, and the expedition had ended in failure before Hatra. Losses in men and machines were heavy. The Parthians had suffered even more. Many of their western cities and territories lay devastated, and death and captivity had reduced the population once again.

Indeed, the signs of exhaustion and decline in the Parthian realm were multiplying. Political stability and central authority had been sadly undermined by generations of dynastic struggles. The destruction wrought by three Roman invasions of Mesopotamia and Babylonia within eighty-five years was incalculable. The spread of the plague no doubt added to the ruin brought by war. Full decadence was now all too apparent in the standard of the emissions of the central government and its dependants; in quality and design the coinage had sunk to appalling depths. The features of the ruler had become little

Plates 6h, k, kk   more than an ill-executed pattern; the originally Greek inscriptions of the reverse had degenerated into total illegibility and now had to be supplemented by Aramaic lettering. In metal and weight, too, earlier numismatic standards were gone. The few official monuments of stone which survive are poorly carved: inscriptions and scenes are alike incompetently done. The

Plate 73   scene in which Khwasak, satrap of Susa, receives the symbol of his office, dated AD 215, is little more than a rough sketch on the stone block. The various incidents that were carved on rock faces at Tang-i Sarvak, Elymais, around AD 200 are little better done, but show events of interest expressed through traditional motifs. One or more kings appear at ceremonies and activities

Plate 74   connected with investiture: divine worship, hunting, military combat and the holding out of the ring of office to two of his vassals.

Slightly better again are the almost certainly late Parthian sculptures found at the shrine of Bard-i Nishandeh, under the threshold of which a foundation deposit of 5,000 Elamite coins was discovered. Among the votive fragments, a relief depicts a local prince worshipping fire; a column from a lower terrace has four persons crudely carved upon it in relief, a practice also found in Roman Syria. But older and higher standards were now seemingly preserved principally in places on the fringes of the Parthian area, at Hatra, at Syrian Palmyra and among the Kushans – with one significant exception. The vassal kings of Persis, from the end of the reign of Vologases V, began to issue a coinage markedly superior in design and quality to the contemporary coinage of their overlord. Had the Arsacids been able to read this omen, they would have recognised the arrival of those who were destined to overthrow them, the heirs of the Achaemenids.

Plate 6p, qq

Vologases V died around AD 207, and was succeeded by his son, Vologases VI (traditionally V). By 213, Vologases' brother, Artabanus V, king of Media, had come out in rebellion and laid claim to Mesopotamia. In 215 he held Susa. The Roman emperor Caracalla took the credit for creating this dispute, and proceeded to provoke war with the Parthians. He seized the sons of the king of Armenia, but in 215 failed to quell the subsequent revolt. In the same year he demanded the surrender of a Cynic philosopher named Antiochus and a certain Tiridates from the Parthians. These having been duly sent, he made a request the following year for the hand of Artabanus' daughter in marriage. This was refused, and gave him the excuse he was so earnestly seeking to march into the 'lands around Media', to destroy fortresses, to seize the city of Arbela, and to open the Parthian royal tombs there and scatter the bones. Coins with the legend Vict(oria) Part(hica) were issued to celebrate this victory. In spring, 217, Artabanus counter-attacked and invaded Roman Mesopotamia. The Romans, embarrassed

Plate 73

*Fig. 48   Graffito representing Papak, king of
Persis* c. AD *210 (after E. Herzfeld,* Iran in the
Ancient East, *fig. 402)*

by the recent assassination of Caracalla, were beaten in a long
engagement and the emperor Macrinus purchased peace for a
huge sum. A further coin issue appeared bearing the same
words Vict(oria) Part(hica).

The end of Arsacid rule was fast approaching. Uncertainty,
however, surrounds the events, which appear in Oriental
sources alone, and archaeology has little to contribute. The rebellion which was to overthrow the Arsacids began in Persis,
theoretically a Parthian vassal kingdom, early in the third century AD. One tradition held that Sasan, ancestor of the Sasanid
line, was a high priest of Anahita at Istakhr, near Persepolis.
His son Papak married the daughter of the local prince and
seized power. This action did not receive the approval of the
Parthian monarch. On Papak's death around the time of Caracalla's invasion, a serious quarrel began to break out between

Fig. 48

his two sons, named Shapur and Ardashir (a later form of Artaxerxes). Shapur, however, was killed by a falling wall, and
Ardashir became king of Persis. A simpler and more likely
tradition, however, makes Sasan a petty ruler of Persis, whose
kingdom was inherited by his son Papak and so eventually by
his son Ardashir. The latter rapidly extended his kingdom
to the north and east. About 220 he broke out into open revolt.
His allies now included Medes, the ruler of Adiabene and king
Domitian of Kirkuk; between them they overran Mesopotamia,
but failed to take Hatra. Artabanus V led the opposition. In
three successive encounters he was defeated, and in the final
battle about 224 or 226 he was killed. Parthia fell into the hands
of Ardashir, who was crowned king in Ctesiphon. Even yet
there was powerful resistance. Vologases VI may possibly have
survived until AD 226/7, and Artabanus' son Artavasdes, who
was striking coins at least as late as this, continued the struggle
for a while from the mountains. Opposition to Ardashir was
maintained in Armenia and elsewhere. But Ardashir was
ultimately triumphant and ordered the carving of a great rock
relief near Firuzabad to commemorate the defeat of Artabanus.   Plate 75
Under the new Sasanid dynasty, which claimed descent from
the Achaemenids, firm government, prosperity and cultural
standards were to return to Iran.

CHAPTER X

Epilogue: Parthian Achievement

THE SURVIVING OFFICIAL RECORDS of the Parthians are surprisingly few. What is more, their history was largely forgotten or obliterated already in the succeeding Sasanian period. This must have been due partly to Sasanian hostility. Furthermore, in Mas'udi's Arabic work *Kitab al-tanbih* we read that Sasanian religious and political leaders artificially reduced Parthian chronology from a period of 510 years to one only half as long. This they did on account of the Zoroastrian belief that the empire of the Persians would end one thousand years after Zoroaster, who was thought to have lived about three hundred years before Alexander. Thus they hoped to postpone this fateful day. Other medieval writers of the Orient also knew of this deception, but many did not and later Zoroastrian tradition allots the Parthians a mere 284 years. But the lack of *contemporary* records of the Parthians is striking. We must not forget the nomadic movement of the Parthian court from capital to capital, the many dynastic struggles, the sackings of Ctesiphon, and the Chinese observation that parchment was the material for writing – all circumstances detrimental to the preservation of documents. Moreover, even a government as well organised as that of the Romans allowed the keeping of its records to become sufficiently chaotic to necessitate the great codifications of laws and edicts by Theodosius and Justinian in the fifth and sixth centuries AD. The Parthian government, through an inadequate preservation of historical records, was probably itself largely to blame for later ignorance.

What developments took place in 'greater Iran' during the half millennium of Parthian rule? When the Parni nomads seized Seleucid territories, they found a land in which Greek civilisation predominated, although many older Oriental traditions survived. This mixed culture and government, far superior to their own, they at first adopted, and under Mithra-dates I and II succeeded in establishing a firm monarchy and a wide empire. The strength of the monarchy, however, thereafter declined, to the political advantage of the nobility. By the first century AD many of the older mixed traditions had been absorb-ed into a new and post-Hellenic phase of Iranian culture, which the Parthians handed on to their Sasanian successors. During Parthian rule, developments in many spheres can be seen. Iranian society, as Frye put it, passed from an ancient to a medieval era. 'Feudalism' of a kind had already been present in Achaemenid Iran. But now we see it emerging clearly, with a weakening central government, a system of noble landlords and oppressed serfs, and a proliferation of titles and insignia. War, hunting, polo, feasting and recitations of epic characterised aristocratic life. The organisation of the army reflected these conditions.

The economic system of the Empire as developed under the Parthians suffered from the disabilities present in most systems of antiquity, but some progress was made. In agriculture, skill in the raising and distribution of water improved. The rise of trade, both internal and international, accompanied the arrival of more peaceful conditions in the first century BC. Cities grew and lived from the profits of the caravans, and the routes of trade now linked the Mediterranean with China by land and sea. The prosperity brought by economic improvement in turn assisted a flourish-ing of the arts. Parthian architects developed a number of im-portant new ideas in the *iwan*, in vaulting and the squinch, and in the decoration of buildings. Parthian art contributed signifi-cantly to future styles. To Roman art the device of frontality and certain motifs probably came from western Parthia, and thence they entered Byzantine art. Sasanian artists took over such Par-thian motifs as the investiture, the seated cross-legged figure and the single combat between horsemen, together with motifs derived originally from Greek art. In these spheres, Hellenism was far from being rejected: it was assimilated into an Oriental way of thinking. In the sphere of religion, Zoroastrianism seems to have continued to spread and to develop towards the form it reached under the Sasanians. But these were achievements of the *subjects* of the Parthians. How far were the Parni responsible for what took place?

The Parthian rulers of Iran are mostly shadowy figures. They seem to have been more interested in their traditional pursuits than in sober government. Their pastimes left few memorials. In many spheres they appear to have shown an admirable tolerance, which was due no doubt to indifference, but which saved their subjects nevertheless from much persecution and oppression. Here and there the guiding hand of the Parthian rulers can be observed, in the leading of their followers to battle and conquest, in the raising of Ctesiphon from a village to a capital, in the sending of ambassadors to the Chinese emperor, or in the collection of Avestan fragments by king Vologases. The basic transformation of the realm from a predominantly Greek to an Iranian society must also have owed much to royal and aristocratic stimulus. But the real achievements of the Parthian monarchs have been obscured by inadequate records and by the Sasanian *damnatio memoriae*. In Iran, recollection of the Parthians faded rapidly, until the poet Firdosi could say, 'I have heard nothing but their names, and I have not seen them in the chronicle of kings.' So that in the Iran of later ages only the memories of a few names and of a violent downfall survived. The characters of Parthian history, where they were remembered at all, were used merely 'to point a moral, and adorn a tale'.

Plate 76

TENTATIVE GENEALOGICAL TABLE OF THE ARSACID KINGS

Parthian spellings of royal names are given in italics within brackets. Vertical lines indicate father to son succession, and horizontal dashes mean blood or adopted brothers. Bracketed numbers after Vologases show the old numbering of the kings, now probably to be revised. (After R. N. Frye, *The Heritage of Persia* ([London 1962], p. 294).

Arsaces I (*'ršk*) 247–? – – – – 'Tiridates' (*tyrdt*)
c. ?–211 BC

Artabanus I (*'rtpn*)
c. 211–191 BC

Priapatius (*prypt*)
c. 191–176 BC

Mithradates I (*mtrdt*) – – – Phraates I (*prdh, prdty*)
c. 171–138 BC   c. 176–171 BC

Phraates II c. 138–128 BC? – – ?Sinatruces (*sntrwk*)   Gotarzes I (*gwtrz*)
c. 78/7–71/0 BC?   c. 91–78 BC?

Artabanus II c. 128–124/3 BC   Orodes I (*wrwd*)
Mithradates II c. 124/3–87 BC   Phraates III c. 70–58/7   c. ?–78 BC?

Orodes II c. 57–38 BC – – – Mithradates III c. 57–55

Phraates IV c. 38/7–2 BC   Tiridates II c. 31–25 BC
Mithradates c. 10 BC

Phraataces (*prdtk*) – – – – Vonones I (*whwnm?*)
c. 2 BC–AD 4   c. AD 7–12
Orodes III c. AD 4–7   Phraates c. AD 35
Artabanus III c. AD 12–38   Tiridates III c. AD 35–6
(Cinnamus c. AD 37?)
Vardanes (*wrt'n*) – – – – Gotarzes II c. AD 38–51   Meherdates AD 49
c. AD 39–47
Vonones II c. AD 51
Vologases I (*wlgš*)   Pacorus II (*pkwr?*)   (Vardanes II?) c. AD 56–58
c. AD 51–80   c. AD 77–115   Artabanus IV
Vologases II AD 78/8, 89/90?   Osroes c. AD 89–128?   c. AD 80–81
Vologases III (II)
c. AD 105–147   Mithradates IV
Vologases IV (III)   c. AD 128–147?
c. AD 148–192
Vologases V (IV)
c. AD 190/1–206/7

Vologases VI (V) – – – – – – Artabanus V
c. AD 207–227?   c. AD 213–224 or 226

Artavasdes (*'rtwzd*)
c. AD 226–7?

Bibliography

Remarkably little has been written about the Parthians; most of this is highly specialized, and in a wide variety of languages. Some useful books and articles are indicated here.

Ancient Authors and texts

GREEK

Principally APPIAN, ARRIAN, DIO CASSIUS, ISIDORUS CHARACENUS, JOSEPHUS, LUCIAN, PHILOSTRATUS, PLUTARCH, POLYBIUS, STRABO.

LATIN

Principally AMMIANUS MARCELLINUS, HORACE, JUSTIN: Epitome of Pompeius Trogus, OROSIUS, PLINY THE ELDER, TACITUS, VELLEIUS PATERCULUS.

ORIENTAL

Principally the AVESTA (translated M. MULLER, Oxford 1883), FIRDOSI (study by T. NOELDEKE, Strasbourg 1904), the HAN-SHU, MAS'UDI, MIRKHOND, MOSES OF CHORENE, TABARI, the TALMUD, YAQUT.

INSCRIPTIONS AND PARCHMENTS

CANTINEAU, J. and STARCKY, J., *Inventaire des inscriptions de Palmyre* (Beyrouth 1930–3, 1949)

CAQUOT, A., (Inscriptions of Hatra), in *Syria* XXX 1953, XL 1963, XLI 1964.

CUMONT, F., (Greek inscriptions of Susa), in *Comptes rendus de l'académie des inscriptions,* 1930–1932.

DURA EUROPOS, *The Excavations: Parchments and Papyri,* by C. A. WELLES, R. O. FINK, J. F. GILLIAM and W. B. HENNING (Final Report V, part I), New Haven 1959.

DYAKONOV, I. M. and LIVSHITS, V. A., *Dokumenty iz Nisy,* Moscow 1960.

HENNING, W. B., *Mitteliranisch, Handbuch der Orientalistik,* Leiden 1958.

MARICQ, A., (Hatra, Trajan, Vologasias) in *Syria* XXXII 1955, and XXXIV–VI, 1957–9.

McDowell, R., *Stamped and Inscribed Objects from Seleucia*, Ann Arbor 1935.

Minns, E.H., 'Parchments...from Avroman', *Journal of Hellenic Studies* XXXV 1915, 22f.

Nyberg, H.S., 'The Pahlavi Documents from Avroman', *Le monde oriental* XVII 1923, 182f.

Robert, L., Collection of Greek inscriptions from Asia (forthcoming).

Rostovtzeff, M.I. and Welles, C.B., 'A Parchment Contract from Dura', *Yale Classical Studies* 2 1931, 46f.

Safar, F., (Inscriptions of Hatra), in *Sumer* VIII–X 1951–1954.

Sznycer, M., 'Ostraca d'époque parthe trouvés à Nisa', *Semitica* V 1955, 65f.

Hellenistic Asia

Bevan, E., *The House of Seleucus,* London 1902.

Bikerman, E., *Les Institutions des Séleucides,* Paris 1938.

Cook, J.M., *The Greeks in the East,* London 1962.

Jones, A.H.M., *The Greek City from Alexander to Justinian,* Oxford 1940.

Narain, A.K., *The Indo-Greeks,* Oxford 1957.

Rostovtzeff, M.I., 'Seleucid Babylonia', *Yale Classical Studies* 3 1932.

—, *The Social and Economic History of the Hellenistic World,* 3 vols., Oxford 1953.

Tarn, W.W. and Griffith, G.T., *Hellenistic Civilisation,* London 1952.

Tarn, W.W., *Hellenistic Military and Naval Developments,* Cambridge 1930.

—, *The Greeks in Bactria and India,* Cambridge 1951.

Parthian History and General

Browne, E.G., *Literary History of Persia,* Cambridge 1951.

The Cambridge Ancient History vols. IX–XI.

Christensen, A., *L'Iran sous les Sassanides,* Copenhagen and Paris 1936.

Debevoise, N.C., *A Political History of Parthia,* Chicago 1938.

Dilleman, L., *Haute Mésopotamie et pays adjacents,* Paris 1962.

Dubs, H.H., *A Roman City in Ancient China,* London 1957.

Frye, R.N., *The Heritage of Persia,* London 1962.

GHIRSHMAN, R., *Iran from the earliest times to the Islamic Conquest*, Harmondsworth 1954.

HERZFELD, E. E., 'Sakastan', *Archäologische Mitteilungen aus Iran* IV 1932.

JUNGE, J., Saka-Studien, Leipzig 1939.

JUSTI, F., *Iranisches Namenbuch*, Marburg 1895.

KAHRSTEDT, U., *Artabanos III*, Berne 1950.

LEPPER, F. A., *Trajan's Parthian War*, Oxford 1948.

MAENCHEN-HELFEN, O., 'The Yüeh-chih Problem re-examined', *Journal of the American Oriental Society* 65 1945, 71–81.

MARQUART, J., *Eransahr*, Berlin 1901.

—, *A Catalogue of the Provincial Capitals of Eranshahr*, Rome 1931.

NODELMAN, S. A., 'A Preliminary History of Characene', *Berytus* XIII 1960, 83f.

WARD PERKINS, J. B., 'The Roman West and the Parthian East', *Proc. of the British Academy* li 1965, 175–199.

RAWLINSON, G., *The Sixth Oriental Monarchy*, London 1873.

SAFAR, F. 'Hatra and the first Season of Excavations', *Sumer* VIII 1952.

SCHMIDT, E., *Flights over Ancient Cities of Iran*, Chicago 1940.

SYKES, P., *A History of Persia*, vol. I, London 1921.

TARN, W. W., 'Seleucid-Parthian Studies', *Proc. of the British Academy* 1930.

WOLSKI, J., 'The Decay of the Iranian Empire of the Seleucids and the Chronology of Parthian Beginnings', *Berytus* 12 1956–7, 35f.

Coins

DAYET, M., 'Monnaies arsacides à bonnet satrapal', *Revue numismatique* XI 1949, 9f.

HILL, G. F., *Catalogue of the Greek Coins of Arabia, Mesopotamia and Persia*, London 1922.

McDOWELL, R. H., *Coins from Seleucia on the Tigris*, Ann Arbor 1935.

NEWELL, E. T., 'The Coinage of the Parthians', in POPE, A. U. (ed.) *A Survey of Persian Art*, Oxford 1938, vol. I, 480f.

Sammlung PETROWICZ, *Arsakiden Münzen*, Vienna 1904.

LE RIDER, G., *Suse sous les Séleucides et les Parthes*, Paris 1965.

SIMONETTA, B., articles in *Numismatica* 1948 and 1953, and in *Numismatic Chronicle* 1949, 237f.

WROTH, W. W., *Catalogue of the Coins of Parthia*, London 1903.

Economics and Society

ECONOMICS

ADAMS, R.McC., *Land Behind Baghdad,* Chicago and London 1965.
AL-HAIK, A., 'The Rabbou'a Galvanic Cell', *Sumer* XX 1964, 103–4.
WHEELER, R.E.M., *Rome Beyond the Imperial Frontiers,* London 1954.
WILL, E., 'Marchands et chefs de caravanes à Palmyre', *Syria* XXXIV 1957, 262f.

POTTERY

DEBEVOISE, N.C., *Parthian Pottery from Seleucia,* Ann Arbor 1934.
ETTINGHAUSEN, R., 'Parthian Pottery', in POPE, A.U.(ed.), *A Survey of Persian Art,* Oxford 1938, vol. I, 646f.
OATES, D. and J., 'Nimrud 1957,' *Iraq* XX 1958, 114f.

JEWELLERY

ACKERMAN, P., 'Parthian Jewellery', in POPE, A.U. (ed.), *A Survey of Persian Art,* Oxford 1938, vol. I.
MACKAY, D., 'The Jewellery of Palmyra and its Significance', *Iraq* XI 1949, 160f.

SILVER

ACKERMAN, P., 'The Art of the Parthian Silver and Goldsmiths', in POPE, A.U.(ed.), *A Survey of Persian Art,* Oxford 1938, vol I.
FRYE, R.N., 'A Parthian Silver Bowl', *Artibus Asiae* XVII 1954, 143–4.
WEITZMANN, K., 'Three Bactrian Silver Vessels with Illustrations from Euripides', *The Art Bulletin* XXV 1943, 289f.

SEALS

DEBEVOISE, N.C., 'Parthian Seals', in POPE, A.U. (ed.), *A Survey of Persian Art* (Oxford 1938), vol. I.
—, 'The essential Characteristics of Parthian and Sassanian Glyptic Art', *Berytus* I 1934, 12f.
MASSON, M.E. and PUGACHENKOVA, G.A., (Parthian seal impressions from Nisa), *Vestnik drevnei istorii* 1954, 4, 159f.

TEXTILES

ACKERMAN, P.,'Parthian Textiles', in POPE A.U. (ed.),*A Survey of Persian Art*, Oxford 1938, vol. I, 685f.
PFISTER, R., *Les textiles de Palmyre,* Paris 1934–40.

EPIC

BOYCE, M.,'The Parthian gosan and the Iranian Minstrel Tradition', *Journal of the Royal Asiatic Society* 1957, 10f.
CHRISTENSEN, A., *Les gestes des rois dans les traditions de l'Iran antique,* Paris 1936.

Religion

DUCHESNE-GUILLEMIN, J., *Zoroastre,* Paris 1948.
DUMÉZIL, G., *L'idéologie tripartite des indo-européeens,* Brussels 1958.
JACKSON, A.W.W., *Zoroaster,* New York 1898, p. 152–7.
MEILLET, A., *La religion indo-européenne,* Paris 1921.
UNVALA, J.M., *Observations on the Religion of the Parthians,* Bombay 1925.
WIKANDER, S., *Feuerpriester in Kleinasien und Iran,* Lund 1946.
ZAEHNER, R.C., *The Dawn and Twilight of Zoroastrianism,* London 1961.

Archaeology

GENERAL

VAN DEN BERGHE, L., *Archéologie de l'Iran ancien,* Leiden 1959.
HERZFELD, E., *Am Tor von Asien,* Berlin 1920.
—, *Archaeological History of Iran,* Oxford 1935.
—, *Iran in the Ancient East,* Oxford 1941.
POPE, A.U. (ed.), *A Survey of Persian Art,* Oxford 1938, vols. I, IV.
ROSTOVTZEFF, M.I., *Caravan Cities,* Oxford 1932.
AUREL STEIN, SIR M., *Old Routes of Western Iran,* London 1940.
—, *Innermost Asia,* Oxford 1928.

SITES

ANDRAE, W., *Hatra,* vols. I and II, Leipzig 1908 and 1912.
ANDRAE W. and LENZEN H.,*Die Partherstadt Assur,* Leipzig 1933.
ANDRAE W., *Das wiedererstandene Assur,* Leipzig 1938.
VAN DEN BERGHE, L., 'Le relief parthe de Hung-i Nauruzi', *Iranica Antiqua* III 1963, 155f.

DURA EUROPOS: *Excavations at Dura Europos* (Preliminary and Final Reports), *edited by* BAUER, P.V.C., ROSTOVTZEFF, M.I., WELLES, C.B. and others, New Haven 1929–.

GHIRSHMAN, R., *Cinq campagnes de fouilles à Suse, 1946–51*, Paris 1952.

HEINRICH, E., 'Sechsten vorläufiger Bericht über die... in Uruk-Warka unternommenen Ausgrabungen', *Abhandlungen der Preussischen Akademie der Wissenschaften*, Berlin 1935.

HINZ, W., 'Zwei neuentdeckte Parthische Felsreliefs', *Iranica Antiqua* III 1963, 169f.

MASSON, M.E., (New data concerning the ancient history of Merv), *Vestnik drevnei istorii* 1951, 4, 89f.

PUGACHENKOVA, G.A., (Architectural monuments of Nisa), *Vestnik drevnei istorii* 1951, 4, 185f.; 1953, 3, 159f.

REUTHER, O., *Die Innenstadt von Babylon (Merkes)*, Leipzig 1926.

SCHLUMBERGER, D., and BERNARD P., 'Aï Khanoum', *Bulletin de Correspondance Hellénique* 79 1965, 590f.

STARCKY, J., *Palmyre (Guide archéologique)*, Beyrouth 1952.

SUSA: Excavations published in *Mémoires de la mission archéologique en Iran*, Mission de Susiane, Paris 1900–.

WATERMAN, L., *Preliminary Report* (and *Second Preliminary Report*) *upon the Excavations at Tel Umar, Iraq*, Ann Arbor, 1931 and 1933.

Architecture

DEBEVOISE, N.C., 'The Origin of Decorative Stucco', *American Journal of Archaeology* XLV 1941, 45f.

HOPKINS, C., 'The Parthian Temple', *Berytus* V 1942, 1–18.

LENZEN, H., 'Architektur der Partherzeit' in *Festschrift* WEICKERT, C., Berlin 1955.

—, 'Ausgrabungen in Hatra', *Archäologische Anzeiger* 1955, 334f.

REUTHER, O., 'Parthian Architecture', in POPE A.U. (ed.), *Survey*, vol. I, 411f.

SHOE, L.T., 'Architectural Mouldings of Dura Europos', *Berytus* IX 1948, 1f.

Art

AVI-YONAH, M., *Oriental Art in Roman Palestine*, Rome 1961.

VAN BUREN, E.D., *Clay Figurines of Babylonia and Assyria*, Yale 1930.

CHABOT, J.B., *Choix d'inscriptions de Palmyre*, Paris 1922.

COLLEDGE, M.A.R., *The art of Palmyra: a historical survey* (forthcoming).

CUMONT, F., *Fouilles de Doura-Europos*, Paris 1926.

DOERNER, F.K. and GOELL, T., *Arsameia am Nymphaios*, Berlin 1963.

GHIRSHMAN, R., 'Bard-è Nechandeh', *Syria* XLI 1964, 301f. and XLII 1965, 289f.

GHIRSMAN, R., *Bégram*, Cairo 1946.

—, *Iran, Parthians and Sassanians*, London 1962.

—, 'Un bas-relief d'Artaban V avec inscription en pehlvi arsacide', *Monuments Piot* 44 1950, 97f.

GOELL, T., 'Nemrud Dagh', *Anatolian Studies* V 1955, 13-14.

HENNING, W.B., 'The Monuments and Inscriptions of Tang-i-Sarvak', *Asia Major* II 1952, 2, 151f.

HOMES-FRÈDERICQ, D., *Hatra et ses sculptures parthes*, Istanbul 1963.

HUMANN, C. and PUCHSTEIN, O., *Reisen in Kleinasien und Nordsyrien*, Berlin 1890.

Illustrated London News, 10 Nov. 1951, 17 Nov. 1951, 18 Dec. 1954, 25 Dec. 1954, 18 June 1955, 4 July 1964, 16 July 1966.

VAN INGEN, W., *Figurines from Seleucia on the Tigris*, Ann Arbor 1939.

INGHOLT H., 'Parthian Sculptures from Hatra', *Memoirs of the Connecticut Academy of Arts and Sciences* XII 1954.

—, *Studier over Palmyrensk Skulptur*, Copenhagen 1928.

MARSHALL, SIR J., *Taxila*, 3 vols. Cambridge 1951.

MASSON, M.E., (New data on Parthian history) *Vestnik drevnei istorii* 1950, 3.

MASSON, M.E., and PUGACHENKOVA, G.A., (Parthian Rhytons from Nisa), Moscow 1956.

MICHALOWSKI, K., *Palmyre, fouilles polonaises 1959-*, Warsaw & Paris 1960-.

MONGAIT, A.L., *Archaeology in the U.S.S.R.*, London 1961.

MOREHART, M., 'Early Sculpture at Palmyra', *Berytus* XII 1956-7, 53f.

ROSTOVTZEFF, M.I., 'Dura and the Problem of Parthian Art', *Yale Classical Studies* V, New Haven 1935, 157f.

—, *Dura Europos and its Art*, Oxford 1938.

—, *Iranians and Greeks in south Russia*, Oxford 1922.

ROWLAND, B., 'Hellenistic Sculpture in Iran', *The Art Quarterly* 18 1955, 174f.

SCHLUMBERGER, D., 'Descendants non méditerranéens de l'art grec', *Syria* XXXVII 1960.

SEYRIG, H., *Antiquités syriennes,* Paris 1934–.

—, 'La grande statue parthe de Shami', Syria XX 1939, 177f.

WILL, E., *Art parthe et art grec,* Paris 1959.

YOUNG, J.H., 'Commagenian Tiaras, Royal and Divine', *American Journal of Archaeology* 68, 1964, 29f.

1

2

3

4

5

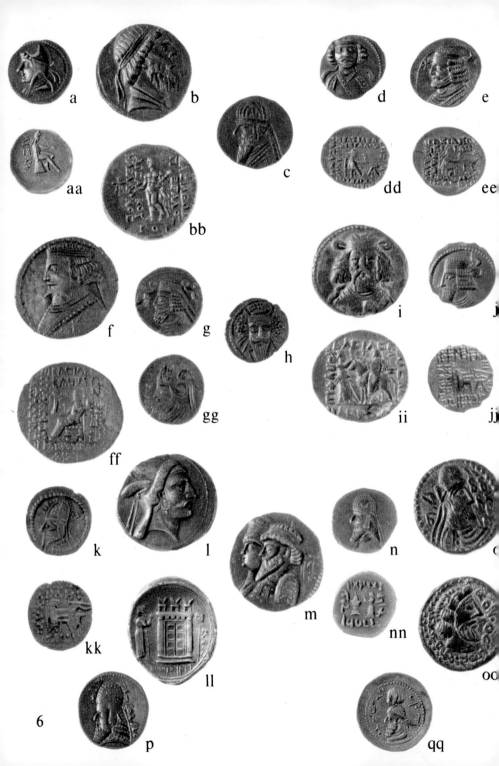

a

aa

b

c

d

e

dd

ee

bb

f

g

h

i

j

ff

gg

ii

jj

k

l

m

n

o

kk

ll

nn

oo

6

p

qq

7

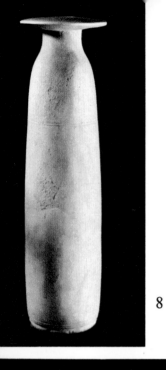

8

9

10

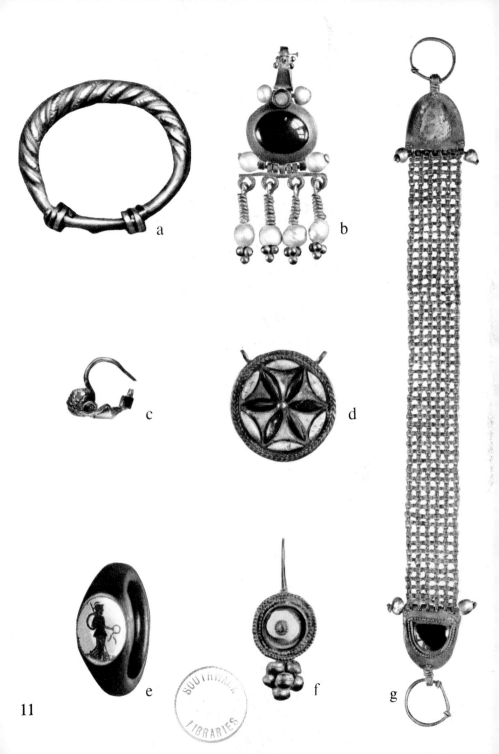

a

b

c

d

e

f

g

11

12

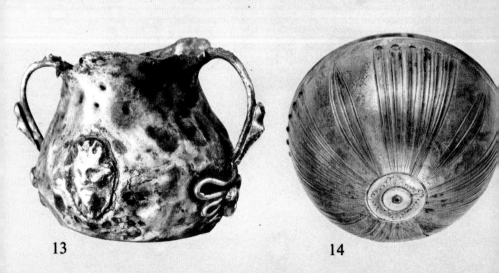

13

14

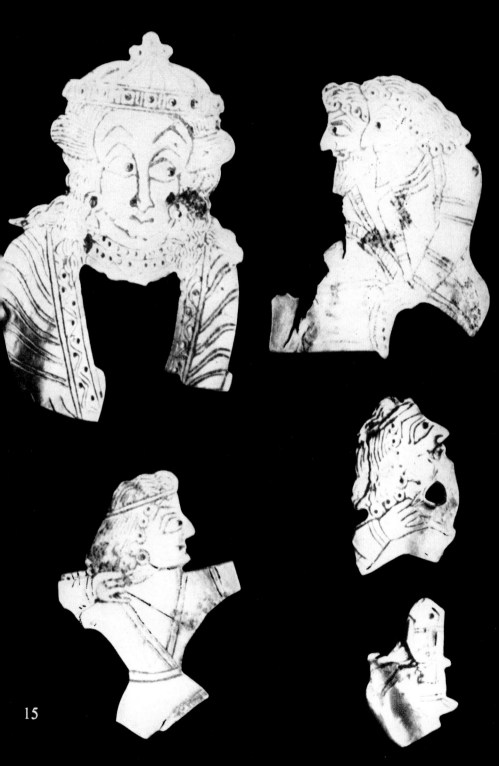

15

16

17

18

19

a

b

c

d

e

20   f

21

22

23

24

25

26

27

a

b

c

d

28

e

29

30

31

32   33

34

35

36

37

40

41

42

43

44

45

46

47

48

49

50

51

52   53

54

55

56

57

58

59

60

61

62

63a

63b

64

65

67

66

68

69

70

71

72

73

74

75

76

بدست یکی مرد خرّاد نام

پیش جهانجوی بر وحش اسیر

کشته شدن از دیوان

رو آمد از اسب شاه از دو

شد ندا اندر پشین کپید و بیک زبان

جو کیرفت بر وحش کرفته کا

ز دور آزد و در از پا پدیارد ش

پیش خیمه از تیر و تیره رو

کرو دشمن پاد شار بهکبیر

ز خشم فرمود شاه اردشی

قلّه بسکالان بر از این کن

خنجر میانش بدنیم کن

زخشم ورکاه فرمان

شد آن نامدار از جهان ناپ

Notes on the Plates

1 Damaged bronze head found at Shami. Fragments of a gold diadem discovered near by indicate that it represented a Seleucid monarch – Antiochus IV Epiphanes, who decreed a cult of himself as divine? Presumably second century BC. Photograph courtesy Teheran Archaeological Museum.

2 Air-view of the Caspian Gates, east of Teheran, which divided eastern Media from western Parthia. The view gives a good idea of the ruggedness of the Elburz range. In the distance may be seen the borders of the Dasht-i Kavir. Courtesy the Oriental Institute, University of Chicago.

3 Restored view of the interior of the central hall within the 'Royal Palace', Old Nisa. The hall was rebuilt a number of times; this shows its approximate state in the first century AD. The walls were divided into two registers and contained niches in which were placed clay figures (of deified royal ancestors?). Courtesy the Editors of *Vestnik drevnei istorii* (1951, 4, 191f., fig. 3).

4 Lower section of the left sarcophagus of the 'Triclinium of Maqqai', a group of three sarcophagi in an underground tomb at Palmyra. Between the legs of the funerary couch, we see Maqqai between two servants, all in Parthian dress, and a horse: he is about to leave for the hunt. Traces of blue and red paint survive. Height of relief about 2 ft 6 in. (76.2 cm.). About AD 229. Still in the Hypogeum of Atenatan, Palmyra. Photograph courtesy the Institut français d'archéologie, Beirut.

5 Parchment written in Aramaic script but in the Parthian or 'Arsacid Pahlavi' language, and discovered with two parchments in Greek at Avroman in Kurdistan. All three documents are concerned with the sale of a local vineyard. Dated to the year 300: *i.e.* 12/11 BC if the Seleucid Era is meant. Photograph courtesy the Society for the Promotion of Hellenic Studies.

6   Coins of the Parthian kings and their vassals (silver, unless otherwise stated). Single letters indicate obverse, double mean reverse. Actual size. Photographs courtesy the Trustees of the British Museum.

a Drachm of Mithradates I, with the head of the king: probably the first Parthian issue to be minted. Around 160–150 BC.

aa Figure of 'seated Arsaces' and Greek legend 'Arsaces'.

b Tetradrachm of Mithradates I in Greek style, produced at Seleucia.

bb Figure of Heracles standing, and Greek inscription which describes Mithradates as Great King and Philhellene, and gives the year 173 (140/39 BC).

c Drachm of Mithradates II depicting the king in the new high royal headdress of the Parthians. On the reverse he styles himself King of Kings. Around 100 BC.

d Drachm with frontal head of 'Mithradates III' (?), 57–55 BC. dd 'Seated Arsaces' and Greek inscription describing him as Great King (only).

e Drachm of Orodes II, who was reigning when Crassus attacked Parthia. *c.* 57–38 BC.

ee The Greek inscription is already blundered.

f Tetradrachm of Phraates IV (37–2 BC), who repulsed Antony's invasion.

ff Phraates styles himself King of Kings and Philhellene. Dated to the (Seleucid) year 280 (33/32 BC).

g Drachm with head of Phraataces.

gg Head of Musa and Greek legend 'The heavenly queen Musa'. AD 2–4.

h Drachm of Vologases V (IV), with frontal head of king in linear style. *c.* AD 190–207.

i Tetradrachm of Artabanus III (*c.* AD 12–38).

ii Artabanus rides a horse – a reference to exile ? – and receives the palm of submission from a city (Seleucia?). The customary royal epithet Philhellene has been deleted. This unusual scene and legend must indicate trouble, now resolved. Dated 338 (AD 26/7).

j Drachm of Vologases I. The Aramaic letters WL indicate his name, as the Greek inscription of the reverse (jj) is almost totally illegible. *c.* AD 51–80.

k Drachm of Artavasdes, last Parthian ruler, with head of king in linear style and Aramaic letters AR (tavasdes). *c.* AD 226/7.

kk The illegible Greek legend is supplemented by one in Aramaic letters which reads 'Artavazi malka'.

l Tetradrachm (obverse) of Bagadat, Seleucid vassal king of Persis in the third century BC.

ll Showing fire-temple and inscription in Aramaic lettering.

m Tetradrachm with portraits of the Parthian 'vassal' king Kamnaskires II and queen Anzaze of Elymais. On the reverse, Greek inscription, figure of seated Zeus and the date 82/1 BC.

n Drachm of the vassal Darius II, son of Autophradates, king of Persis, in headdress of Parthian type. First century BC.

nn Fire-altar, worshipper and legend in Aramaic lettering.

o Bronze tetradrachm of the vassal Maga, king of Mesene/Characene c. AD 195–210, with headdress of Parthian type.

oo With bearded head.

p Drachm with head of Shapur, son of Papak, king of Persis around AD 210–215; Aramaic lettering for legend. Sasanian artistic style is already visible.

qq Drachm (reverse) of Shapur of Persis (c. AD 210–215), with head (of his father Papak?) in royal headdress. Aramaic lettering for legend. Sasanian style is plainly developing.

7 Air-view of Susa. Photograph courtesy the Oriental Institute, University of Chicago.

8 Marble vase from Susa with flared lip. Ht 9 3/4 in. (25 cm.). Parthian period. Photography courtesy Teheran Archaeological Museum.

9 Green-glazed pottery jug of the late Parthian period from Iraq. It has three handles and three face-masks. The shape is a distant offshoot from the Greek amphora. Ht 10 5/8 in (27 cm.). Second or third century AD. Photograph Staatliche Museen, Berlin-Dahlem, Islamische Abteilung.

10 Red terracotta rhyton or drinking-cup with the fore-parts of an ibex from Demavend, Iran. Ht 14½ in. (36.8 cm.), diameter of rim 4 1/4 in. (10.5 cm.). Second or first century BC. Teheran Archaeological Museum. Photograph courtesy the Museo Nazionale d'arte orientale, Rome.

11 Jewellery of the Parthian period.

a Silver bracelet with granulations, as worn on Plate 42. Diam. 3 in. (7 cm.). From Dura Europos. Photograph courtesy Dura Europos Publications.

b Earring with multiple pendants: oval, bar, chains and pearls. Ht. 2 1/4 in. (5.7 cm.).

c Earring. Ht 1 in. (2.5 cm.).

d Brooch with geometrical design. Diam. 1 1/8 in. (2.8 cm.).

e Ring with inset engraved stone bearing the figure of a goddess. Diam. 1 in. (2.5 cm.).

f Earring, ending in 'grape cluster'. Ht 1 5/8 in. (4.2 cm.).

g Bracelet: wires interlock to form an open mesh. At each end a solid plate; wire rings as clasp. Length 7 15/16 in. (18.7 cm.).

b–g from Seleucia on the Tigris, showing Greek influence. Photographs courtesy the Directorate General of Antiquities, Baghdad.

12 Shallow bowl or plate of silver from the Oxus Treasure, in the so-called 'Bactrian' style. The Greek god Dionysus reclines on a chariot. Beside him is Ariadne, and revellers escort him. The technique anticipates Sasanian work: figures in repoussé on separate pieces of metal are attached to the vessel. *Cf.* O.M. Dalton, *The Treasure of the Oxus,* 2 ed., p. 49. Photograph courtesy the Trustees of the British Museum.

13 Silver bowl, with elaborate handles and a decorative head added in repoussé. Found somewhere in Iran. Ht 2 1/8 in. (5.5 cm.), diam. 3 3/4 in. (9.5 cm.). Hellenistic or early Parthian. Photograph courtesy Teheran Archaeological Museum.

14 Silver bowl, partially gilt, from a hoard found near Nihavand, Iran. This hemispherical form has developed out of the older lotus cup type. The exterior is finely decorated with a vine motif. The Greek letters PXA which appear on the bowl may indicate owner or weight. Diam. 5 5/8 in. (14.3 cm.). Datable to the first or second century AD by Roman coins found with it. Photograph courtesy Staatliche Museen, Berlin, Antiken Abteilung.

15 Pieces of the decoration in mother-of-pearl of a box, found at Shami, west Iran. Probably about 100 BC to AD 100. Teheran Archaeological Museum.

16 Bronze figurine of a nude woman from Iran; votive, and probably represents the goddess Anahita, whose cult was significant from the Achaemenian period onwards. Ht 4½ in. (11.5 cm.). First to third centuries AD. Photograph courtesy Staatliche Museen, Berlin-Dahlem, Islamische Abteilung.

17 Bone figurines from Seleucia, representing a nude goddess, and mass-produced for religious purposes. Approximately actual size. Parthian era. Photograph courtesy the Directorate General of Antiquities, Baghdad.

18 Air-view of Takht-i Sulaiman, the ancient Shiz, in Azerbaijan, Iran. The site was probably a holy place even before the Parthian era, although there is no archaeological evidence datable before the early Sasanian period, when the site became a centre of pilgrimage. Photograph courtesy the Oriental Institute, University of Chicago.

19 Terracotta relief made from a mould bought at Aleppo, Syria. A Parthian noble or official stands before a goddess who is framed in a niche, wears basically Greek costume and raises her right hand in benediction. Ht 4 15/16 in. (12.5 cm.). Late Parthian period. Photograph courtesy Staatliche Museen, Berlin-Dahlem, Islamische Abteilung.

20 Figurines for use as religious dedications etc.
a Terracotta horseman. Ht 3½ in. (9 cm.).
c Terracotta torso of bearded man in conical headdress. Ht 3 in. (7.5 cm.).
e Female head in elaborate headdress. Ht. 1 in. (2.5 cm.).
f Female reclining figure with inlaid eyes. Length about 4 in. (10 cm.).
From Seleucia. Photographs courtesy Directorate General of Antiquities, Baghdad.
b Terracotta horseman. Ht about 9 in. (23 cm.). Provenance unknown. Photograph courtesy National Museum, Copenhagen.
d Terracotta figure of woman playing lyre. Ht about 6 in. (15 cm.).
From Iran. Photograph courtesy Teheran Archaeological Museum.

21 Limestone hexagonal altar for the burning of incense, from Palmyra. Decoration includes the Assyrian stepped-merlon motif and Graeco-Roman mouldings. Ht 29 1/4 in. (74 cm.). Damascus Museum. Photograph courtesy the Directorate General of Antiquities and Museums, Damascus.

22 Sarcophagus of green-glazed terracotta found at Uruk/Warka, Iraq, with a decoration of panels in each of which a 'nude soldier' appears. Length 6 ft 5 in. (1.95 m.). Late Parthian period. Photograph courtesy the Trustees of the British Museum.

23 Ruins of the *iwans* of the Sun sanctuary, Hatra, before restoration. Across the middle ground ran the wall which divided the court in front of the *iwans*, and to the left of the centre may be seen the ruins of the south *iwan*, flanked by lesser *iwan* halls. Decorative half-columns and the heads and busts of divinities around the arches are visible. Probably late first or early second century AD. Photograph courtesy the Directorate General of Antiquities, Baghdad.

24 Panel of decorative stucco-work from the 'palace' of Kuh-i Khwaja, Seistan, showing Greek and Oriental motifs. Probably first centuy AD. From E. Herzfeld, *Iran in the Ancient East* (Oxford 1941), plate XCIX.

25 Interior of the corridor which entirely surrounds the square inner shrine of Shamash, attached to the back of the south *iwan*, Hatra, before restoration work. Second century AD. Photograph courtesy the Directorate General of Antiquities, Bagdad.

26 Funerary tower of Elahbel, Palmyra. Inside, there is a decorated hall and a staircase leading to the top, with recesses for sarcophagi on every floor. Several other towers are equally well preserved. The date, April AD 113, is given in an Aramaic inscription on the exterior. Photograph M. A. R. Colledge.

27 Reconstruction of the stuccoed façade of the west *iwan* of the 'Palace' at Assur. The façade was originally painted in bright colours. First century AD. Photograph courtesy the Staatliche Museen, Berlin, Vorderasiatisches Museum.

28 Bronze figurines of Hellenistic style found at Nihavand, west Iran. Perhaps a sanctuary stood near by. Third or second century BC. Photographs courtesy the Teheran Archaeological Museum.
a Statuette of Demeter. Ht 4 in. (10 cm.). b Statuette of Athena. Ht 2 1/8 in. (5.5 cm.). c Figure of young rider. Ht 2 3/4 in. (7 cm.). d Female figure in Greek *chiton*. Ht 3 1/8 in. (8 cm.). e Statuette of Zeus. Ht 5 1/8 in. (13 cm.).

29 East terrace of tomb of king Antiochus I of Commagene (69–34 BC) on Nemrud Dagh, southern Anatolia. Colossal statues of guardian deities,

many times life-size, are built up from huge superimposed blocks of stone. From left to right: king Antiochus himself, the goddess Tyche of Commagene, Zeus-Oromasdes, Apollo-Mithras-Helios-Hermes and Artagnes-Heracles-Ares. Photograph courtesy T. Goell and F. K. Doerner.

30 Relief of king Mithradates Kallinikos or more likely Antiochus I of Commagene (69–34 BC) shaking hands with the god Artagnes-Heracles-Ares, found at Arsameia on the Nymphaeus, below Nemrud Dagh. The king wears the 'Armenian' tiara and an elaborately decorated costume with leggings bound by straps. Heracles is easily identifiable by his lion-skin. Height 7 ft 5 in. (2.26 m.). Photograph courtesy Theresa Goell and F. K. Doerner.

31 Colossal head of the god Apollo-Mithras-Helios-Hermes from the east terrace of the tomb of Antiochus I on Nemrud Dagh. The head of the god is clearly influenced by Hellenistic Greek style, but he wears the 'Persian' tiara. Ht about 8 ft (2.50 m.). Photograph courtesy Theresa Goell.

32 Funerary relief of a bearded man, from the Gate House, Assur. He appears in profile, wears Parthian dress and carries a branch, symbolic of sanctity, like that held by the dead of Palmyra. To the right of his head astral symbols appear. Ht 5 ft 7 in. (1.71 m.). Found with a similar relief dated 89/8 BC. Photograph courtesy the Istanbul Archaeological Museum.

33 Limestone funerary statue of a priest, found in the tomb-tower known as Qasr el-abiad, Palmyra. He wears tunic, cloak, trousers and leggings, and once carried ritual utensils. The ornament and patterning of the drapery are well executed. Life-size. About AD 100. Palmyra Museum. Photograph courtesy the Institut français d'archéologie, Beirut.

34 Religious relief depicting the six Genii of Bet-Phasiel, a village northwest of Palmyra, and a goddess before a worshipper who throws incense on to a burner. The Genii, identified in the Aramaic inscription, are identically clad in tunics, cloaks and 'sarongs' and carry spears and shields. Dated AD 191. Damascus Museum. Photograph courtesy the Institut français d'archéologie, Beirut.

35 Religious relief on a stone beam of the temple of Bel, Palmyra. An Arab religious procession is in progress, shown in the frontal convention. To the right, totally veiled women look on. Then a camel carries a *qobba* containing a holy object, led by a driver who is in turn preceded by a donkey. On the left, more spectators look at the proceedings, in two registers. Ht about 8 ft (2.50 m.). About AD 32. *Sub situ*. Photograph M. A. R. Colledge.

36 Religious relief on a stone beam of the temple of Bel, Palmyra, showing the handshake between two gods, Aglibol and Malakbel, beside altars heaped with fruits of the earth. Aglibol, the moon god, sports a full Hellenistic cuirass over his oriental tunic and trousers. On the right, a small Corinthian temple, and on the left, two attendants (probably in full profile) are included. Ht about 6 ft (1.83 m.). About AD 32. *Sub situ*. Photograph M. A. R. Colledge.

37 Interior of the recess or *exedra* of Iarhai from an underground tomb, Palmyra, reconstructed in the Damascus Museum with the original materials. Each funerary bust closed up the end of a coffin slotted into place behind it. In the niche at the far end can be seen a 'triclinium' or group of three sarcophagi carved in the form of funerary couches with representations of priests and their families on the lids. Ht about 15 ft (4.50 m.). The view shows the recess as it was in the early third century AD. Photograph courtesy the Institut français d'archéologie, Beirut.

38 Religious relief from near Palmyra showing an offering of incense to two 'rider-gods' – Abgal and Ashar, on camel and horse. The composition is frontal and 'heraldic'. The gods are well armed; their puffy hairstyles are Parthian. The snake and stars constitute further religious symbols. The Aramaic inscription records the dedication and the date, October AD 154. Photograph courtesy the Institut français d'archéologie, Beirut.

39 Religious relief from the court of the temple of Bel, Palmyra, with the triad of Baalshamin (in the centre) and the two lesser gods Aglibol (the moon god) and Malakbel. All three wear cuirasses of Hellenistic form over Oriental tunics and trousers, and are placed frontally. The relief is covered with inscriptions cut by the faithful. Ht 22 in. (56 cm.), width 27

in. (68.5 cm.). About AD 50. Paris, Louvre. Photograph courtesy the Service de Documentation photographique des musées nationaux.

40   Limestone head from a funerary bust of Palmyra (PS 235 – Group IIC – in H. Ingholt, *Studier*). Eastern Roman and Parthian styles are fused here. The hair, beard style and slight schematization of the features are Parthian, whereas the facial modelling shows Roman influence. Ht 10 3/4 in. (27.5 cm.). Late second century AD. Photograph courtesy the Trustees of the British Museum.

41   Limestone funerary bust of a cameleer from Palmyra. The huge, penetrating eyes and schematized hair and drapery are characteristic of developed Parthian art. In his left hand he holds a document. Ht 22½ in. (57 cm.). About AD 140–160. Photograph Ny Carlsberg Glyptotek, Copenhagen.

42   Limestone funerary bust of a bejewelled woman, the so-called 'Beauty of Palmyra'. This fine piece illustrates the Oriental sculptors' love of rich detail and ornament. Numerous traces of yellow, red and black paint survive. She had red lips, black hair, a pink patch on each cheek and coloured jewellery. Ht 21 5/8 in. (55 cm.). Early third century AD. Photograph courtesy Ny Carlsberg Glyptotek, Copenhagen.

43   Limestone funerary relief of a married couple from Palmyra (PS 59 in H. Ingholt, *Studier*). The woman carries a spindle and distaff, and has a key hanging from her brooch, to indicate her domestic activities. The inscription between them is false. Ht 18 7/8 in. (48 cm.). About AD 130–150. Photograph courtesy Ny Carlsberg Glyptotek, Copenhagen.

44   Limestone funerary relief of two children from Palmyra (PS 514 in H. Ingholt, *Studier*). They wear embroidered tunics, trousers and extra leggings. The Aramaic inscriptions record that they are Taime (to the right) and his brother Filinus, the sons of Wahballat. The bird and grapes have funerary significance. Ht about 20 in. (50 cm.). About AD 150. Photograph courtesy Ny Carlsberg Glyptotek, Copenhagen.

45   Funerary relief of limestone, showing an elegantly dressed woman before a curtain, from Palmyra (PS 43 in H. Ingholt, *Studier*). Some eastern

Roman influence in the modelling. Some of her jewellery has affinities with that shown in plate 11. The Aramaic inscription gives her name and lineage: she is Aha, the daughter of Halapta. Ht 24 in. (61 cm.). Dated September, AD 161. Photograph courtesy the Museum of the American University of Beirut.

46 Large funerary relief of high-quality limestone, one of a group of three found in the tomb of Malku, Palmyra. We see a Palmyrene family on the funerary couch, with further members shown as busts between the legs. The bowls and leaf held by the man must be connected with the Palmyrene mortuary cult. The eyes of the figures are picked out with black paint. Ht 6 ft 4 in. (1.92 m.), width 6 ft 7 in. (2.01 m.). Early third century AD. Damascus Museum. Photograph courtesy the Directorate General of Antiquities and Museums, Damascus.

47 Bronze head of the statue from Shami shown in plate 51. Photograph courtesy the Teheran Archaeological Museum.

48 Polished marble head of a Parthian prince, vassal or chieftain from Shami. Ht 4½ in. (11.5 cm.). Perhaps about 100 BC–AD 100. Photograph courtesy the Teheran Archaeological Museum.

49 Small bronze bust of a Parthian ruler from Iran. Probably the finial of a sceptre or a piece of furniture ornament. The head resembles coin portraits of Orodes III (c. AD 4–7). Ht 2 3/4 in. (7 cm.). Photograph courtesy Staatliche Museen, Berlin-Dahlem, Islamische Abteilung.

50 Larger than life-size head of king Uthal of Hatra, found in temple III. He wears the high tiara characteristic of Arsacid monarchs and widely imitated by their vassals. Beard and features are stylized. Ht 24 5/8 in. (62.5 cm.). Second century AD. Mosul Museum. Photograph courtesy the Directorate General of Antiquities, Baghdad.

51 Bronze statue, probably of a Parthian vassal ruler, from Shami. Head and body were cast separately. The costume is almost identical to that in plate 33. Fine detail is engraved on the torque and belt, and lines indicate hair on the beard and chest. Ht 6 ft 6 in. (2 m.). About 50 BC–AD 100. Teheran Archaeological Museum. Photograph courtesy M. Anvar.

52   Slightly larger than life-size marble statue of a king of Hatra. Ht 7 ft 1 in.
      (2.15 m.). Second century AD. Photograph courtesy the Directorate General of Antiquities, Baghdad.

53   Life-size marble statue of the princess *dwšpry* (Dawashfari?), daughter of
      king Sanatruq of Hatra, from temple V. She stands in an attitude of
      worship, richly dressed, in a high turban and with an abundance of jew-
      ellery. The Aramaic inscription on the base gives details of her name and
      lineage, and the date (AD 137). Ht 7 ft (2.10 m). Iraq Museum, Baghdad.
      Photograph courtesy the Directorate General of Antiquities, Baghdad.

54   Life-size marble statue of the god Ashur-Bel found in temple V, Hatra.
      The god is flanked by two eagles of Hatra and Tyche, the Spirit of the
      City, sits at his feet. The Greek cuirass and the figure of Tyche are borrow-
      ed from Hellenistic art, whereas the beard is almost Assyrian. The statue
      is lightly polished in places. Ht about 4 ft (1.20 m.). Probably later first
      or second century AD. Iraq Museum. Photograph courtesy the Director-
      ate General of Antiquities, Baghdad.

55   Pair of marble statues representing a noble and his wife (or god and god-
      dess) of Hatra. They wear the usual elaborate costumes of the Hatrene
      aristocracy. The eyes are inlaid to give a greater intensity of gaze, by ancient
      oriental custom. Ht of man 34 5/8 in. (88 cm.) and of woman 33 7/8 in.
      (86 cm.). Iraq Museum, Baghdad. Photograph courtesy the Director-
      ate General of Antiquities, Baghdad.

56   Religious relief of the Eagle and Standard of Hatra, and the Sun God,
      found side by side in a Hatrene temple, and inscribed in Aramaic. First or
      second century AD. Mosul Museum. Photograph courtesy the Directorate
      General of Antiquities, Baghdad.

57   Plaque from Hatra with the head of Medusa. Ht 4 in. (10.5 cm.). Prob-
      ably second century AD. Iraq Museum, Baghdad. Photograph courtesy
      the Directorate General of Antiquities, Baghdad.

58   Bronze eagle, worshipped at Hatra. Ht 3 in. (7.6 cm.). First or second
      century AD. Iraq Museum, Baghdad. Photograph courtesy the Director-
      ate General of Antiquities, Baghdad.

59 Bronze statuette of Heracles-Nergal from Hatra. The modelling of the figure, which has been borrowed from Greek art, has been schematised. Ht 6 7/8 in. (17.5 cm.). Probably second century AD. Iraq Museum. Photograph courtesy the Directorate Genral of Antiquities, Baghdad.

60 Religious relief of the goddess Allat between two acolytes above a lion, from Hatra. The figure of Allat is imitated from the Athena of Greek art, but transmuted into Parthian style. The two lesser goddesses raise their right hand in blessing. Ht 51 in. (1.28 m.). Iraq Museum. Photograph courtesy the Directorate General of Antiquities, Baghdad.

61 Religious relief from Hatra. Four deities in curious headgear hold an assortment of fruits of the earth. Inlaid eyes create an intensity of expres-sion. Ht 13 3/4 in. (35 cm.). Probably second century AD. Photograph courtesy the Directorate General of Antiquities, Baghdad.

62 Circular alabaster plaque from Hatra with a bust of the Moon goddess above the crescent moon in relief. The goddess looks surprisingly Greek. Ht 14 1/8 in. (36 cm.). First or second century AD. Photograph courtesy the Directorate General of Antiquities, Baghdad.

63 Two alabaster figurines of gods of Hatra. Probably second century AD.
a Male god, with Aramaic inscription. Ht 11 3/4 in. (30 cm.).
b Sun god in attitude of benediction. Restored ht 7 in. (19 cm.).
Photographs courtesy the Directorate General of Antiquities, Baghdad.

64 Sculptured limestone lintel of a temple at Hatra. In the centre, a god re-clines, holding a bowl and attended by two winged Victories and other figures. An arch rose above this flat lintel. Width about 8 ft 3 in. (2.50 m.). Late first or second century AD. Iraq Museum. Photograph courtesy the Directorate General of Antiquities, Baghdad.

65 Upper section of a larger than life-size marble statue of king Sanatruq of Hatra, from temple X. He wears an elaborately decorated tunic (sewn with pearls?), a collar, belt and trousers. The Eagle of Hatra adorns his diadem. His right hand is raised in worship. Total ht 7 ft 4 in. (2.24 m.). Early second century AD. Iraq Museum, Baghdad. Photograph courtesy the Directorate General of Antiquities, Baghdad.

66 Limestone archivolt figure, from an arch on the façades of the *iwans* of
the Sun sanctuary, Hatra. We see the upper half of a Moon goddess or of
Anahita above the crescent moon. Ht 2 ft 4 5/16 in. (72 cm.). Late first or
second century AD. Photograph courtesy the Staatliche Museen, Berlin-
Dahlem, Islamische Abteilung.

67 Religious relief: the stele of Aphlad from Dura Europos. A priest in a
conical hat throws incense on to a burner before the god, who faces the
front wearing a cuirass of Hellenistic type. A Greek inscription contains
the dedication and date, AD 54. Photograph courtesy Dura Europos
Publications, Yale University.

68 Interior of the south *iwan* of the Sun sanctuary, Hatra, before restoration
work. Above the doorway can be seen a pilaster decorated with three
theatre masks of Graeco-Roman type, probably with ritual significance.
On the right, the back wall and the doorway into the shrine of Shamash.
Late first or second century AD. Photograph courtesy the Directorate General of Antiquities, Baghdad.

69 Wall painting of the god Mithras as hunter on horseback, in the Mithra-
eum of Dura Europos. He wears standard Parthian costume, and the
technique of the paintings is predominantly linear, although Romans
now occupied the town. Around AD 200. Photograph courtesy Dura
Europos Publications, Yale University.

70 Wall painting in the 'Temple of the Palmyrene Gods', Dura Europos,
with part of the scene known as the 'Sacrifice of Conon', now destroyed.
Two priests in conical hats, carrying ritual equipment and assisted by an
attendant, are throwing incense on to burners. About AD 75. From F.
Cumont, *Fouilles de Doura Europos,* Paris 1926, plate XXXII.

71 Wall painting of three frontal gods in the Long Gallery of the 'Palace' of
Kuh-i Khwaja, Seistan. Strong influence from Hellenistic Greek art is
present, but the gods shown are Indo-Iranian. Probably first century AD.
From E. Herzfeld, *Iran in the Ancient East,* Oxford 1941, pl. CIV.

72 Head of a queen or goddess found at Susa, of inferior white marble streaked

with grey. The sculptor, Antiochus the son of Dryas, who has signed his name across the diadem, has given the head a soft or 'blurred' finish. If the diadem indicates a queen, this may represent Musa, wife of Phraates IV and co-regent with Phraataces, and belong to the years AD 2-4. The plastic indication of the pupils of the eye and the light surface polish, however, point to a later date, and the head may rather represent the Tyche (Spirit) of Susa. Ht 14 3/4 in. (37.5 cm.). First (or earlier second?) century AD. Teheran Archaeological Museum. Photograph courtesy M. Anvar.

73 Inscribed limestone (funerary?) relief from Susa. King Artabanus V hands the ring of office to Khwasak, satrap of Susa. Very low relief and poor execution, but an important historical document nevertheless: Susa has returned from Elymaean to royal Arsacid government. Dated 14 September, AD 215. Photograph courtesy the Teheran Archaeological Museum.

74 Rock relief at Tang-i Sarvak, Elymais. Badly weathered, but historically important. Reliefs on the rock faces show scenes connected with investiture. Here Orodes, local ruler of Elymais, reclines on a couch and holds out the ring of office to two of his vassals. The Aramaic inscription above is written in the local version of the Aramaic script. Probably *c.* AD 200. Photograph courtesy the Teheran Archaeological Museum.

75 Early Sasanian rock relief at Firuzabad, showing the defeat of Artabanus V by Ardashir, in AD 224 or 226. Artabanus may be seen to the far right, falling backwards off his horse to a spearthrust from the Sasanian. Heraldic emblems distinguish the combatants. Ht about 11 ft (3.35 m.). AD 225-50. Photograph courtesy the Herzfeld Archives, Freer Gallery of Art, Washington 25, DC.

76 Indian miniature of the Moghul period in a manuscript of the *Shahnameh* of Firdosi. Ardawan (Artabanus V), on foot, is being put to death by Ardashir on horseback to the right. AD 1602. Photograph courtesy the Metropolitan Museum of Art, New York, Gift of Alexander Smith Cochrane, 1913.

Index

235